Better Homes and Ga

Making
Beautiful
Gardens

Text by Roger Mann
Photographs by Lorna Rose

MURDOCH BOOKS®

Sydney • London • Vancouver • New York

CONTENTS

Garden styles 42

The functional garden 90

STARTING OUT

To create something beautiful—and maybe to touch the hearts of those we love with its beauty—is one of the deepest joys life can offer. It isn't given to all of us to compose symphonies or create masterpieces of painting or sculpture, but anyone can create a beautiful garden. The pictures in this book bear witness to that. The gardens range from large country places to small city ones; none is the garden of a palace, and all (or almost all) have been created by their owners.

These gardens represent many styles, for there are as many ways to make a garden beautiful as there are gardeners. Some, no doubt, will not be to your taste; others, maybe, will be gardens to dream about. And that is the first step: to dream.

Making your garden dreams come true is not difficult—growing plants is not a difficult craft. If you have ever decorated a room to your satisfaction then you have already mastered the basic skills of design—skills in working with colour, proportions, creating harmony, and in adapting other people's great ideas to suit yourself. In some ways, garden-making is easier, for unlike furniture and carpets, plants are always beautiful in themselves.

Think of the garden as an outdoor room or a series of rooms. The earth is its floor and the sky its roof; trees, fences, maybe the façade of the house will be its enclosing 'walls'; shrubs and flowers are its furniture and accessories. And just as you do when you are laying out a room, you begin by taking stock of what you have to work with, taking note of both its good points and its drawbacks. Consider how much land you have to play with; whether it is sloping or more or less level; which way it faces, into or away from the sun and breeze. How will you enter the garden from the house and from the street? Do you have a pleasing outlook which you can frame with trees (to create a

LEFT: This late-spring garden features the cool tones of blue, purple and white. Notice how the repetition of vertically arranged flowers such as delphiniums, campanulas, salvias and lavender unites the whole picture. The frame of grey foliage could equally well set off a bonfire of vivid red and orange flowers such as cannas, geraniums and scarlet salvias.

OPPOSITE: Part of the joy of a garden lies in the legends that have grown up around so many flowers. The Greeks told of Narcissus, the vain youth whom the gods transformed into a flower to punish him for neglecting a lovelorn nymph—and here that flower is in a late-spring garden. The colour of its centres is echoed by the orange geums. Over all wave the honey-scented blossoms of a flowering plum.

PLANNING A GARDEN

Sentiment can play a great part in planning a garden: everyone has favourite plants and flowers that they remember and love from their mother's garden, from a previous garden of their own, or by association with a particular friend or loved one. By all means, plan to include them in your designs but make sure they are suited to your soil and climate. If they aren't and don't grow well, it can be heartbreaking. If they do, they can add a special and personal touch to your garden.

window as it were) or are there things like fences or the neighbours' houses that you will want to screen from view? Have you inherited trees or other plantings from a previous owner? And, most importantly, how much time are you prepared to spend on gardening?

DEVELOPING A PLAN

Shifting trees, rocks and soil around to see how they fit in is much more difficult than shifting furniture so it's a good idea to sketch your ideas out first. Use tracing paper to save messing up your original plan. Concentrate at first on the big picture—where to put your trees, the driveway, patio and lawn: fill in the details later. (You don't have to be an artist—even the roughest sketch can help clarify your ideas.) As you develop your sketches, keep an open mind. Often something that seems to be a liability can turn into an advantage. An awkward slope may become the starting point for an interesting change of levels; the trees that you had to plant for privacy might set the theme for the whole garden.

Your soil and climate will determine the range of plants you have to play with but don't let that cramp your style. Too warm for tulips? Iceland poppies can give the same splash of warm spring colour. Too cool to drape the house in bougainvillea? How about climbing roses instead? Nor should you be frustrated if you don't have a great deal of time to devote to gardening. Gardens designed for low maintenance (maintenance-free gardens don't exist any more than housework-free homes do) can be just as beautiful in their simplicity as more intricate, demanding ones. In any case, it is always wise to keep the main lines of your design bold and uncluttered. Plants add their own intricacy of leaf and flower, and you can add embellishments as the garden grows. But remember, don't try to do everything at once!

Creating a beautiful garden takes time, and time is on your side. So while you work, take some time off to enjoy the flowers—isn't that what a garden is for?

THREE STEPS TO A BEAUTIFUL GARDEN

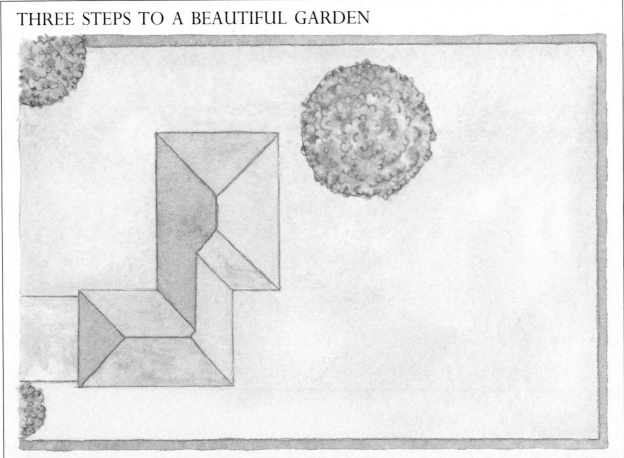

I Draw a plan showing the outline of your garden, adding the existing structures and other large features such as trees or shrubs.

2 Sketch in the main features of your design—the paving, grass, trees and shrubs.

3 Add a few final touches to the plan—this is what your garden will look like.

USING COLOUR

olour is an essential part of a garden's impact—few gardens look their best in a black and white photograph—and playing with colour is one of the most enjoyable things about gardening. The very fact that flowers are fleeting is part of the fun: you can change your colour schemes to suit your fancy and the changing seasons. You might, for instance, go for gold in spring with daffodils, pansies and wattle, and then change to cool blue and white for summer, using, say, blue petunias and lobelia, agapanthus and white daisies. Just about every colour you could desire can be found in flowers, limited only by your own taste and sense of what goes with what. (If in doubt, try picking a flower and holding it up against its proposed companions to see how it will look.)

Not that you should try to be as precise in your garden colour-scheming as you are indoors: flowers are not always that predictable in colour (chances are, each of your blue petunias will be a slightly different shade); they don't always come into bloom precisely on schedule; and their colour is almost always diluted with the green of their own leaves and those of other plants nearby. Your golden springtime scheme is in fact a green and gold one, but no less cheerful for that.

ABOVE: The simplest of pictures—spring flowering trees set against a background of evergreens, with a seat placed for easy admiration. These dogwoods (*Cornus florida*) will have a second season of colour in autumn when their leaves turn scarlet. Dogwoods are for cool districts only, but in warm ones, you could create a similar picture with white bauhinias.

LEFT: By tradition, pale colours are feminine and romantic. Although they can look washed-out in the glare of high summer, they are especially appropriate to spring. Here is an old-fashioned planting in cream, mauve and pale pink, its cool delicacy enhanced by the greyish leaves of the white valerian (*Centranthus*) in the foreground, its informality by the way the flowers casually spill over the gravel path.

COLOUR WHEEL

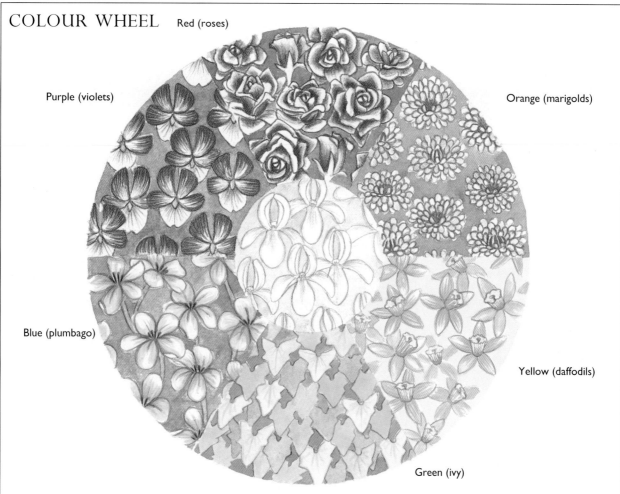

Red (roses)

Purple (violets)

Orange (marigolds)

Blue (plumbago)

Yellow (daffodils)

Green (ivy)

Joining the rainbow into a circle tells us a lot about colour relationships. Those on opposite sides contrast, each intensifying the other when placed together; those adjacent blend and harmonise. Notice how the warm colours, red and orange, are opposite green, which is why these flowers stand out so brilliantly in the garden. Pink and coral are diluted red and orange, and similarly, appear brighter when placed against a green background. You can exploit this effect by placing warm colours in the foreground and cooler blue tones beyond to enhance the effect of distance.

LEFT: A green and white colour scheme in the garden always looks cool and elegant. Here a white lilac, an iris or two, and a viburnum sparkle against a tapestry of varied greens.

PLANT COLOURS

Every gardener has his or her own way of describing colours. What one might call magenta is shocking pink to another, so if the precise colour of a new plant is important to you, always try to see it (or a good photograph) before you buy.

Shrubs that flower before their leaves appear, or so abundantly that they hide them, can be difficult to handle. Their sheer mass of colour can easily upstage more discreet companions, and without green to buffer them, they can easily clash with each other. No problem of that here: the soft, cool pink of the tamarisk and the vivid blue of the ceanothus go happily together. Both bloom in late spring.

Nature knows what she is doing: green is the most flattering background for flowers, much more so than the hard (and usually ill-assorted) colours of brick walls, concrete paving and fences. The first step in creating a colourful garden is the establishment of its green frame by planting trees, clothing fences and walls with creepers, and softening the edges of driveways and pavements with low foliage. This done, the garden will always be pleasing, even at times when there are no flowers. The eye finds green the most restful colour of all, and an all-green garden can be an oasis of tranquillity amid the stresses of modern life.

Easiest of all gardens to maintain, the all-green garden needn't be boring, for foliage offers an almost infinite range of tones from the limpid pale ones of spring through to the deeper shades of summer, from emerald through olive to grey-green. Nor will it always be without flowers. Many trees and shrubs offer them in due season, and of course, you can add as many bulbs, annuals and perennials as you desire—and have the time to look after.

Maintenance is an important factor when planning for colour: keeping up a year-round display of flowers does take dedication. If time and enthusiasm are short, you might like to follow the old tradition of concentrating your efforts on one glorious season of flower, perhaps the spring, then allowing the garden to revert to green for the remainder of the year with just a few bright flowers at focal points. (It is a course well worth considering in dry-summer climates where drought and water shortages can make a summer display difficult.)

There are fashions in flower colours, as there are in clothes and decoration, but there is no need to follow them. If you prefer bright contrasting colours to the currently fashionable romantic blends of soft tones— pinks, mauves and pale blues—by all means indulge in them. Don't allow yourself to be too rigid in your colour-scheming either. You might decide on a blue and white theme—but might just a touch of pink or pale yellow make it sparkle? If you want to mix and match every colour that the season offers, why not? It's your garden, and it's there for your enjoyment.

ABOVE: There is a surprising number of green flowers, though their tone is usually lime or yellowish green rather than emerald. They can look very sophisticated with blue or lavender, as here where a clump of *Euphorbia wulfenii* is set off by a single mauve iris. The sword-like leaves of the iris and the more intricately textured foliage of the euphorbia are almost the same shade of greyish green.

ABOVE RIGHT: Hot, clashing colours like these can be very exciting, but you wouldn't use them in the living room—you'd be tired of them in three weeks! In the garden it's a different story:

the flame of the autumn foliage and the magenta of *Erica canaliculata* will only last about that time. Then you can look forward to them next year. Notice how evergreens frame each colour, making the effect still more brilliant.

BELOW: When using contrasting colours—here orange and purple— it is best to use them in unequal quantities so that one provides the melody, so to speak, and the other the accompaniment. In this beautifully balanced arrangement of lavender and Iceland poppies, the greyish leaves of the lavender soften the contrast.

ELEMENTS OF THE GARDEN

A successful garden is more than the sum of its parts—but it makes the task of creating one easier if you consider the various parts separately, at least in the beginning. Think of the floor, the ground itself and of covering it with grass, groundcovers or paving; of paths that cross it and link the various sections together; of the fences, hedges and trees that enclose and shelter the garden; and of the gates that are its doorways. All these elements work together to create the whole—and when they have been considered and arranged to your satisfaction, add the finishing touches such as garden furniture and ornaments.

An elegantly simple composition of shrubs, trees and a long bed of spring flowers, mostly foxgloves, are striking features of this garden. A cedar and a few azaleas separate this part of the garden from the area next to the house without interrupting the flow of space.

COVERING THE GROUND

The earth is the floor of the garden but bare dirt, dusty in dry weather, muddy in wet, is hardly a satisfactory surface. It needs to be clothed, and the simplest way to do this is the one nature usually uses—a carpet of grass or low-growing plants.

Grass is in many ways the ideal garden floor: it is relatively cheap and easy to lay; you can walk and play on it; it absorbs glare and the sound of footsteps; and its even green is the perfect foil for trees and flowers,

unifying the whole design in much the same way a well-chosen carpet does a room.

Grass is a groundcover, but the term usually means other low-growing plants that grow dense enough to keep out weeds and maybe provide flowers in season. They come into their own in places where grass would be impractical—odd corners too small to mow, shady areas, or wherever you want a green carpet but it isn't important that you be able to walk.

ABOVE: In a cool climate, English lawn daisies are allowed to grow among the grass, to spangle it with white and turn it into a flowering meadow. The shasta daisies in the foreground pick up the theme, and the whole picture is nicely set against a backdrop of trees. In warmer climates, clover could provide the white flowers as well as help the lawn stay green in summer.

LEFT: A simple sweep of grass sets off the deep greens of hedges and the autumn gold of deciduous trees. Notice how the grass flows right up to the dense evergreen shrubs and how their branches sweep the ground. The mower can be tucked in underneath them and no hand-trimming of the grass edges is needed.

TOP: Groundcovers always look best when the planting is kept simple. Here spring-flowering trees rise from a luxuriant carpet of *Epimedium alpinum*, whose leaves, though evergreen, turn bronze in winter. It is best in a cool, not-too-dry climate.

BOTTOM: A lawn as immaculately maintained as this one is a splendid feature in its own right. You would no more cut it up with flower beds or 'specimen' trees than you would scatter furniture all over a fine Persian carpet.

GARDEN PATHS

Whether they be grass, gravel, paved with brick or stone, straight or curved, your paths will have a major impact on the appearance and mood of the garden, and here aesthetics, function and economy go hand in hand. You don't want your garden crisscrossed with paths like a Union Jack; but on the other hand, you do want to have a safe, comfortable passage (no tripping over irregularly laid stones or ducking wet foliage) from one part of the garden to the other. Paths should always lead somewhere definite—even if it is only to a seat or a statue. If you don't really need a path, leave it out: the garden will almost always look better without unnecessary features.

A path running between masses of planting can be grass but usually paths are paved. Concrete and bitumen (asphalt) are too tainted by their association with the city to look well in a garden, so the choice is usually gravel, brick or stone, depending on budget and taste.

ABOVE LEFT: Paths should always be generous in width, especially when, as pictured, plants are allowed to encroach on their edges. A metre and a half path allows two people to walk and talk side by side. The surface here is gravel, an ideal material for an informal setting, though it needs regular raking to keep it looking its best.
ABOVE RIGHT: A narrow paved path leading through luxuriant planting can have a charm of its own but it still shouldn't be uncomfortably narrow. At a metre or so, this path is about the right width. The surface is brick, which lends itself as well to informal treatments as to more formal ones. Concrete bricks are better than clay ones in shaded situations as they aren't quite so liable to get slippery with algae in wet weather. A wash with copper sulphate or swimming-pool chlorine will control the problem, at least temporarily.

LEFT: Here the path curves to follow the contours of the ground, with the uphill slope held by a low stone retaining wall. The low hedge on the right contrasts with the free-growing trees and shrubs on the other side, and also acts as a fence to keep people from straying off the path and falling down the hill.

PLANNING A PATH

Paths don't have to be straight; often a curving route is a more pleasant one. Ensure your curves are generous; not wriggling. Test them by setting them out with string or the garden hose and walking them in both directions. Curved paths always look more natural if they skirt some obstacle such as a tree, a clump of shrubs, or even a large rock. This needn't have been there first of course, and if it conceals the destination as you approach, it can add an air of mystery to the journey.

While some paths look best when allowed to naturally blend into the foliage a more formal path can be enhanced by edging—bricks, tiles or wooden planks are popular.

TYPES OF EDGING FOR A PATH

Stone strip

Plain tile

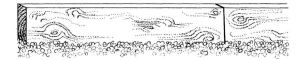

Plank strip

Dragon's tooth

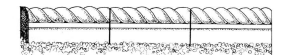

Rope topped tile

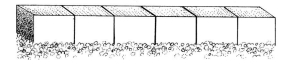

Upright brick

BRICK PAVING

Just as there are rooms in a house for which carpet is not the floor surface of choice, there are situations in the garden where grass is insufficiently hard-wearing and groundcover plantings are not appropriate. Here, on driveways, paths or places where we entertain, a paved area provides us with a firm, dry surface underfoot and, in many cases, acts as an extension of our indoor living area.

While bricks and clay pavers are hard-wearing and non-skid, other materials such as gravel, concrete, stone or wood blocks are popular alternatives. Second-hand house bricks are inexpensive and lend a rustic atmosphere to the garden, but as with all pavers, they reflect heat and glare and can be uncomfortable in hot weather. To combat this, shade large areas of paving with shrubs, trees or vine-clad pergolas.

ABOVE: Brick need not be laid in straight lines; it can also be laid in sweeping curves. The groundcover is ivy, kept under control by regular trimming.

LEFT: Choosing the same brick for the screen wall, the paving and the raised beds gives unity to this shaded patio. You could play down the formality of the design by changing the clipped box hedge to plants that would casually spill out over the edges of the beds. As it is, the restrained colour scheme of green, gold and grey foliage and white flowers (impatiens and *Zephyranthes candida*) sets off the neutral tone of the bricks rather well.

PATTERNS FOR BRICK PAVING

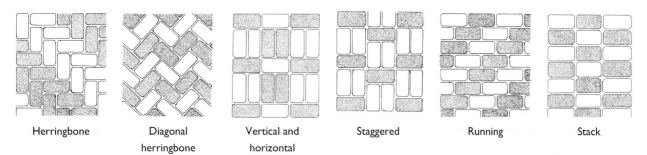

Herringbone   Diagonal herringbone   Vertical and horizontal   Staggered   Running   Stack

Running and circular

ABOVE: A curved path needs to be a little wider than a straight one for comfortable walking. Here the curves of the path are not so tight that the bricks had to be cut to conform.

ABOVE: Pointing up the joints with cement is not obligatory. Here they are simply filled with sand and the grass encouraged to grow between the bricks to soften the formality of the straight lines.

STONE PAVING

Stone has always been a favourite material for garden construction, for retaining walls, steps and paving. Of the many kinds of stone—sandstone, granite, slate, limestone or marble—the best and often the cheapest is usually the local one that underlies your own ground.

Stone is a versatile paving material. Cut in square and rectangular slabs and laid precisely with the narrowest of joints, it can be severely formal or, shaped roughly and fitted like a jigsaw puzzle (crazy paving), it can be as informal and rustic as you could wish. Freshly cut, many stones look raw and hard in colour but dirt and the weather soften them quite quickly—mellowed stone can give a garden a beautiful air of having been there forever. The harder, finer grained stones such as slate and marble can take a high polish, but keep such stones for flooring indoors as they can get dangerously slippery in the rain. A slightly textured, non-slip finish is essential in the garden.

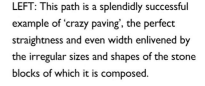

LEFT: This path is a splendidly successful example of 'crazy paving', the perfect straightness and even width enlivened by the irregular sizes and shapes of the stone blocks of which it is composed.

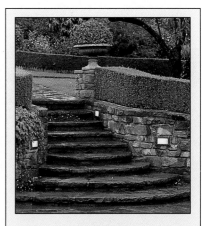

STEPS

Often one part of the garden is at a higher or lower level than the next, and here you need steps to get safely from one level to the next. Stone steps always look handsome, but you can use any of the materials you use for ordinary paving. Make the ascent a gentle one, gentler than indoors, with each step not more than 15 cm high and comfortably deep. An odd number is easier to take in your stride, but try not to have just one. It is easy not to notice one step until you have tripped over it!

ABOVE: Constant traffic across a lawn can wear out the grass, leaving an ugly track. A path is called for, but a solid strip of paving cutting the lawn in half is hardly elegant. Stepping stones, made from either stone or square concrete slabs, can be an attractive compromise.

ABOVE: Precast concrete slabs, cheap and easy to lay, can be useful where you need a path to give you access for tending plantings. If your needs change, they are easily taken up for use elsewhere.

LAYING STEPPING STONES

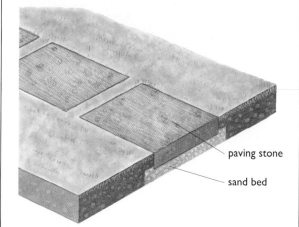

paving stone

sand bed

Paving stones, whether they are fitted closely in a path or set apart, need a firm bed or they'll wobble and become unsafe. Thinly cut paving slabs are best set on an 8 or 10 cm thick bed of concrete; thicker stones can be set on a 10 cm bed of sand, well rolled and tamped down for firmness. When laying stepping stones across grass, first lay them out across the grass to get the spacing right and then strip the turf and remove the soil to allow for a sand bed for each stone, a bit bigger than the stone itself. Place the stone firmly, and replace the turf, cutting to fit.

HEDGES

Until very recently only the rich could afford to enclose their gardens with walls or fences. Common people took cuttings of some suitable shrub and planted a hedge. Today, hedges remain one of the most economical and attractive ways to enclose a country garden. Waist high, a hedge will keep out dogs and children; head high or taller, it provides privacy and greatly attenuates the noise of traffic.

Clipped to shape, a hedge literally becomes a green wall, almost as much a work of architecture as of gardening. Not all hedges need to be clipped: an informal flowering hedge can be beautiful too. Any shrub that grows bushy to the ground can be used: camellias, oleanders, azaleas, plumbago, *Rosa rugosa*, grevilleas, lavender or correas. Where space is tight, it is better to plan for a clipped hedge from the start.

ABOVE: There is no backdrop so flattering for a planting of assorted flowers as the velvet of a perfectly clipped coniferous hedge. Yew is the classic, though it is not for climates with hot summers; this hedge is of *Cupressus torulosa*.

LEFT: The formal lines of this clipped *Lonicera nitida* hedge take the place of a front fence. Star of the planting here is the pale pink *Malus ioensis* 'Plena', last of the crab-apple trees to bloom in spring.

ABOVE: Though some people dislike the smell of its freshly trimmed branches, box is one of the best choices for a clipped hedge whether ankle high or the shoulder height of this one. Whether you choose the European box (*Buxus sempervirens*) or the Japanese (*B. japonica*) depends on climate: the European likes a cold winter, the Japanese a mild one. Both are unhappy in the tropics, where the larger leaved *Duranta repens* does duty. It might be a bit prickly for this situation, however.

SHAPING A HEDGE

While we think of formal hedges as having vertical sides, it is a mistake to try to trim them exactly vertical. Not only is it difficult to judge an exact vertical line but as the hedge usually grows wider at the top, it won't be long before the sides slope outwards. The result is that the lower parts get starved for light and die off. It's much better to trim to an inward slope to prevent this from happening. It need not be as pronounced as the diagrams show—but it shouldn't be less than 10 degrees.

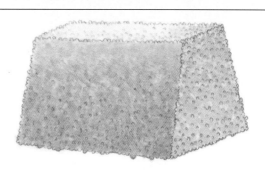

Narrowed box hedge

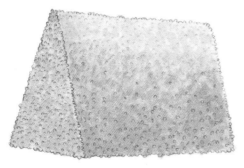

Pyramid hedge

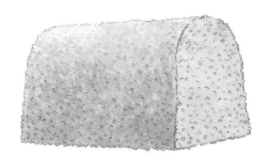

Rounded hedge

GATES

Gates are the doorways of the garden, and like the doors of a house they can be attractive focal points in the design of the garden.

A gate is not an isolated ornament: it should harmonise with the surrounding wall, fence or hedge. Sometimes the logical thing to do is to match gate and fence in material and detail—a picket gate in a picket fence. Or by contrast, setting a delicate wrought iron gate in a massive masonry wall can enhance its elegance. The style of both house and garden will play its part also. An informal garden might be announced by a rustic gate, a formal garden by one more finely crafted; a Victorian house asks for a traditional style in both gate and front fence. The mistake to avoid is the gate that looks stronger and more impenetrable than the barrier though which it gives access.

ABOVE: Here the gate exactly matches the picket fence—itself without fancy elaboration—and the entry to the garden is given sufficient emphasis by painting it a different colour (green, to match the letter box) and carefully flanking it with symmetrical plantings of Japanese maples inside the fence and clumps of agapanthus on the outside. The whole effect is charming and elegant rather than magnificent, a perfect prelude to the informal garden beyond.

LEFT: There is really no pressing need for a gate here—this is a path from one part of a fairly large garden to another—but it heightens your curiosity as to what you will find when you open it and pass through, and it does keep the dog out of the vegetable patch. Its rustic simplicity is in perfect harmony with its surroundings. Whether you hang a gate so it opens to the left or the right depends on which is more comfortable in the particular case though it is best to have the gate open 'inwards', that is, away from you.

TYPES OF GATES

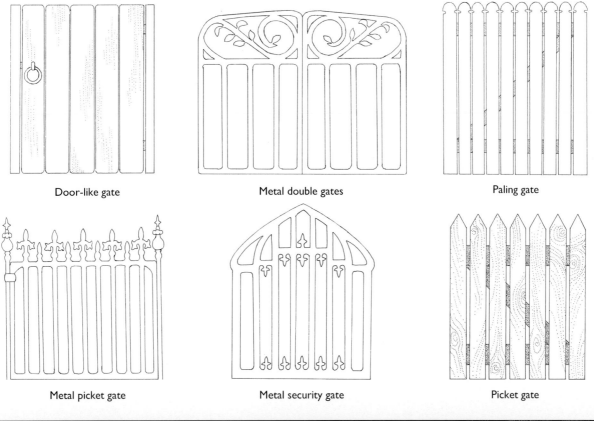

Door-like gate

Metal double gates

Paling gate

Metal picket gate

Metal security gate

Picket gate

ABOVE: You can't see the house from here, but the scale and splendour of its metal gates suggest it is not going to turn out to be a two-room cottage! The gate is saved from ostentation by the way its massive piers are set in a matching wall and by the luxuriant planting of cypresses, wisteria and ornamental grapes, which almost hide its magnificence. Notice how well the large vehicle gate and the small pedestrian gate on the left are brought into one design.

FENCES AND SCREENS

The prime purpose of a fence is to keep out the neighbours, human or livestock, or at least to mark the boundaries of the property. By tradition, front fences allow a view of the house, and back and side fences are expected to provide some degree of privacy. Economy usually precludes them being tall enough to hide neighbouring houses and enforces the use of the cheapest materials (timber palings or corrugated iron, according to local fashion), so they are rarely handsome either.

The most obvious way to improve matters is to beautify the fence itself. You might paint it an olive green or dark brown to camouflage it, rebuild it to a more pleasing design, or cover it with climbing plants— the garden equivalent of wallpaper. By strategically placing trees and shrubs along the fence you can block out unwanted views of houses, power lines or traffic, while still allowing views of the sky and trees beyond. The fence then recedes into the shadows making the garden seem more spacious and private.

In places where front fences are not allowed, privacy from the street can be a problem. Here a planting of shrubs and flowers immediately in front of the verandah serves the same purpose as the pierced window-screens of Indian palaces, allowing the inhabitants to see what is happening in the street while they remain invisible.

ABOVE: Here the stuccoed brick wall, with its beautifully proportioned openings, is the main feature—a garden room indeed. You could clothe the wall with creepers and plant flowers at its foot but the severely simple treatment here emphasises the richness of the garden beyond. The tree is a silver birch in autumn dress.

ABOVE: The need for privacy doesn't always mean you need to build a fence that will obliterate the sight of the neighbours' house altogether. In this case, all that is masked are the windows, leaving the handsome lichen-covered roof to play its part in the picture against the trees beyond.

TYPES OF FENCES

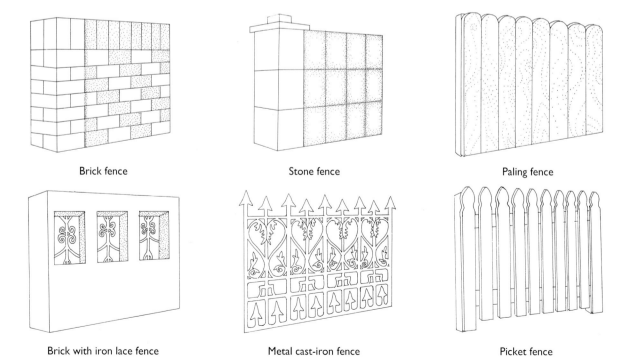

Brick fence

Stone fence

Paling fence

Brick with iron lace fence

Metal cast-iron fence

Picket fence

FRAMING THE VIEW

The Japanese have a phrase, 'borrowed scenery', to describe using trees or hedges to block out undesirable elements in the view from the garden—houses or a road, perhaps—while leaving a distant mountain or the trees on a neighbour's land visible. While the garden might be small, this 'borrowing' of scenery allows it to gain a great feeling of spaciousness.

We can do that too: but we can also frame the view more tightly, as though we were creating a window in the walls of our garden room. We might place sentinel trees whose branches form an arch, or we might actually build an arch or a pergola. Sometimes the window might actually be a door, through which we can pass into another garden room glimpsed from the first. In this case, we might take the opportunity to design our two garden rooms in contrasting manners—one more formal or colourful than the other. The possibilities are endless.

ABOVE: Don't forget the view of the garden from inside the house. Here a window frames the vista of a brick path flanked by azaleas and camellias. (From the garden, the window forms the terminus of the reverse vista.) The path doesn't actually lead into the house: just before it arrives, it takes a right-angled turn and proceeds parallel to the wall.

ABOVE: An ogee-roofed pavilion, half hidden by foliage, turns out on closer approach to shelter a gate into a second garden, complete with swimming pool, whose existence was concealed until now. Surprises like this can be delightful, but don't try for too many or the garden will feel restless. Unless you are gardening on a very grand scale, one is enough.

LEFT: Framing the view between two areas of the garden allows us to create two garden rooms each with completely different functions—one may be designed for more intensive gardening, the other for low maintenance. In this picture the view is concealed until the last moment; then, when you pass through the laburnum-clad arch, you come across a small paved garden. A little further along, a wider arch clad in roses frames the view of a second, informal garden, larger than the first—all in the compass of an average-sized suburban garden!

PLANNING AN ARCH

It is a common mistake to make a garden arch too low and narrow, forgetting that climbing plants grow out as well as up, narrowing your passageway. Don't make an arch less than a metre and a half wide, with the height in due proportion. This is important if you plan to clothe your arch in roses, whose thorns can inflict serious injury.

TYPES OF ARCHES

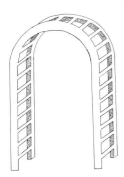

Round-topped arch

Flat-topped arch

Apex arch

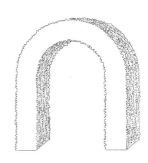

Hedge archway

PERGOLAS

The sky is the roof of the garden but beautiful as the clouds and the stars are, its immensity is hardly intimate. A pergola, a structure of beams supported by posts or columns, not only provides shade but when clothed with scented vines—roses, wisteria or jasmine—it becomes a romantic bower.

Usually constructed from timber, either left in its natural state or dressed and painted, pergolas can also be made with steel, brick or stone columns. The advantage of a pergola is that you can tailor its size to fit the space you want to cover. Shade cloth or closely spaced battens can provide instant shade but the foliage of climbing plants is more usual and delightful. A pergola is a blend of architecture and horticulture—pave the area beneath, add furniture and shade-loving plants, and you will have a perfect extension of your indoor living space.

It is said that the badge of a true artist is the way he turns the unplanned to an advantage. Here is an instance: the rose was originally planted to cover the pergola but has been allowed to ramble into the adjacent liquidambar also, mantling both in fragrant pale pink blossoms. In the foreground, pinks (*Dianthus plumarius*) echo its colour.

ABOVE: A pergola is built over this path but is only an incident along the way: would it look better had the whole length of the path been covered, so that in spring you walked down a tunnel of fragrant wisteria blossoms and in the summer your whole journey was shaded from the sun? The two vines here could easily clothe a pergola twice as long as this.

LEFT: Another free-standing pergola, again clothed in wisteria, but built this time from massive, unsquared timbers, gives a rustic effect quite different from the fine-lined formality of the one above. Wisteria is the classic pergola vine as it considerately hangs its flowers below the roof for you to enjoy. It casts excellent summer shade and then drops its leaves to let in the winter sun. While wisteria is very common, just about any vine can be used to clothe a pergola, but think carefully before you choose thorny growers such as roses or bougainvillea—poking your head up among thorny branches at pruning time is no fun!

BOTTOM LEFT: This pergola marks the transition between the hedge-enclosed gravelled area and the lawn and flower garden beyond. It will be clad with wisteria in a few years to provide a welcome pool of shade in a basically sunny garden.

SHADE TREES

Useful and beautiful as pergolas can be, most gardeners will consider that trees are the most beautiful way to provide a canopy over the garden.

Shade trees need to be placed with care. A tree doesn't cast shade mostly on the area immediately beneath it the way a pergola does. It has height as well as spread, and it can throw its shadow quite a long way when the sun is low. That may be a good thing or it may not. You won't be pleased if your vegetable patch is cast into unwanted shade; on the other hand, you may welcome the afternoon shade cast across the lawn by a tree growing on the other side of the garden.

The density of the shade varies with the species, an important factor to consider when selecting your trees. Eucalypts, birches and the flamboyant tree (*Delonix regia*) are among those that cast only light shade; most rainforest trees and conifers are much denser, the mango often being considered the shadiest of all trees.

ABOVE: A driveway shaded by an avenue of majestic trees can be a very memorable feature of a country garden. The trees are pin oaks (*Quercus palustris*) underplanted with agapanthus.
TOP LEFT: Planting smallish trees in an avenue gives them importance, especially when they are young, allowing you to create shade without having one tree dominating the garden. These are Japanese cherries (*Prunus serrulata*), a foam of pale pink in spring. The pink flowers are *Nerine bowdenii*, a South African bulb.
BOTTOM LEFT: A swing hanging from a sturdy bough is one of the delights of childhood—and a temptation to adults as well. Don't the trees make a beautiful frame for the view of the water? The swing tree is an English oak (*Quercus robur*), a tree for cool climates.

SHADY GARDENS

Trees can provide shade for the garden but choose them carefully. Do you want one large shade tree or several small ones?

One large tree provides shade for a medium-sized garden but dominates the design.

A number of smaller trees can provide an equal amount of shade. If deciduous, they'll also let in the winter sun.

GARDEN SEATS

Some gardeners are content to sit on the grass or on a step and see no need for furniture. Others prefer to include a seat or two, placing them to give a choice of sitting in the sun or in the shade.

Whether you go for traditional or modern styling, garden seats that stay outside all the time need to be strong and durable as well as comfortable. The best timbers are cedar, oak and teak, none of which needs painting. Stone and Victorian iron lace can look very grand though they are cold and hard to sit on. Plastic is modern and popular and wicker furniture can look charmingly Edwardian, but both of these quickly weaken by constant exposure to the rain and sunlight. Whatever your preferred style, the charm of a garden seat is its invitation to sit awhile and forget the cares of the world.

Victorian designs in cast iron and wood are, surprisingly, not extremely heavy. This is an advantage when the seat is simply set on the grass, as here. You can shift it out of the way at mowing time or to a nearby spot if frequent use begins to wear out the grass.

ABOVE: Made to a design by Sir Edwin Lutyens, this seat is so magnificent it is almost a throne and would be the focal point of any garden in which it was placed. Notice how it is backed up against a substantial planting, in this case rambler roses and evergreens. This should be done wherever possible, as not only do few seats look good from behind, but most people feel uncomfortable sitting with their backs exposed.

BELOW LEFT: A sturdy seat in teak is placed in this garden to allow leisurely enjoyment of the spring flowers. Teak is one of the most durable of all timbers, but even it will eventually rot if placed in direct contact with the damp ground. Here the freely draining gravel of the path provides a dry footing.

BELOW RIGHT: Setting a seat on a panel of paving not only prevents the problem of worn-out grass, it gives the seat an air of importance, almost as though it were on a dais. Notice how the paving is set flush with the ground so that the mower can easily run over it, obviating the need for hand-trimming the edge. This is another Victorian design.

SCULPTURE

Gardens have been adorned with sculpture ever since the days of the Romans and a statue, carefully chosen and placed, can still add a touch of distinction to the garden. These days, we are not confined to gods and goddesses, cherubs or lions. If you want to call a birdbath, a Japanese lantern or a handsome piece of pottery a sculpture, then go ahead. You might even feature a large and unusually shaped rock as is often done in Chinese gardens.

Sculpture just asks to be made the focal point of the garden picture, positioned at the end of a path, against a backdrop of greenery, by the side of a pool, or as a relief sculpture mounted on a wall. The size of your sculpture depends on the distance from which it will be viewed. If in doubt, always err on the side of having it too big: you can always play it down by half-submerging it in greenery, but it's almost impossible for a tiny piece of sculpture to make any significant impact.

ABOVE: A really fine piece like this bronze faun deserves to be placed where you can admire it from all around—but you still need to ensure that it is facing its audience. Here the setting of low-growing flowers is just right, but there is a path approaching from behind; should it be blocked off with more planting?

While you might not want to put your sculpture on a pedestal, it does need to be given a stable, secure footing, either concrete or brick. Bolt it in place if there is any possibility of its being accidentally knocked over or stolen.

LEFT: Cement reproductions of antique sculpture are widely available and not very costly. This sculpture looks quite at home embowered in flowers against the simple backcloth of a brick wall. That the flowers match her creamy colour is a nice touch.

LEFT: There is a nice touch of humour here in the way the two geese are placed at the edge of the pond, as though they had wandered into the garden in the hope of catching a fish. The edges of the pond are not completely masked by planting so that you can easily attend to any maintenance and be able to enjoy watching the fish.

AGEING CEMENT

Any well-made piece of cement sculpture can look fine once it has weathered and aged. The impatient can try washing the sculpture with a mix of yoghurt and water to encourage the growth of moss and lichen. Others have been known to attack their statues with a hammer, chipping areas such as the edges of the drapery folds to make them look antique. If a statue is genuinely ancient, the accidents of history can add to its charm, but they are very difficult to fake convincingly so don't try unless you are sure you know what you are doing.

SUNDIALS

Sundials are an obsolete way to tell the time, but watching the shadow of the gnomon, or pointer, pass across the dial gives a sense of contact with the workings of the universe. As it has to be placed outdoors, a sundial can make a charming centre-piece in the garden. Many sundials are not very eye-catching though there are styles that are splendid pieces of abstract sculpture. However, a pretty sundial that does not work properly can be very annoying so ensure that yours has been made for your latitude, and that it is set up with the gnomon pointing exactly north. It will record 'real', not daylight-saving time.

POTS AND POT PLANTS

If you truly want a low-maintenance garden, avoid pot plants. A plant in a pot always needs much more attention than the same plant growing in the open ground. It cannot search for water and nourishment, and so needs regular watering and fertilising. So, why would a garden-owner want to grow plants in pots?

There are many reasons. A pot allows you to grow plants in areas where soil is not available: on the verandah, a paved patio, on a balcony or along a path. Pot plants are portable, which means you can have flowering plants in key positions where you want flowers all the time (as a welcome display for visitors by the front door). It is often easier to achieve this with pots than trying for an all-year display in one garden bed. For people who are renting, potted plants have an added advantage—they can move when you do.

A plant gains an air of importance when you grow it in a pot, in much the same way as a statue does when you place it on a pedestal. For the novice gardener, growing a plant in a pot and tending to it daily can be a very enjoyable way to learn about its habits and needs.

ABOVE: We don't often think of using cut flowers in the garden, and a vase of carnations might look a bit silly, but don't these camellias look charming floating in their antique Japanese bowl? You could place a similar arrangement by the front door to welcome guests, or scatter smaller pots of floating flowers around the garden for special outdoor occasions.
LEFT: Pots don't need to be fancy. These two box bushes are hardly big enough yet to frame the view down the path but raised off the ground in terracotta pots, they gain immeasurably in importance.
OPPOSITE: While we usually place potted plants on a paved surface, there is no reason why a splendid plant cannot be stood on the lawn—though if it is to be a temporary feature it shouldn't stay there for more than a week lest it be remembered by a patch of dead grass. The container is artificial stone and is about as big as can be conveniently moved.

FOCAL POINTS

The eye doesn't like to wander aimlessly across what it sees—it is happiest if presented with some centre of interest, a focal point, on which it can rest and to which it can return as it explores the rest of the view.

In a room, a focal point might be a bunch of bright flowers or a mirror over the mantelpiece. In a garden, it may be simply the point to which the main lines of the composition lead. In a formal, symmetrical plan the focal point is usually the centre, but even in the most informal layout the lines of a path lead the eye to its end (or to a place where it changes direction).

There are many ways to create a focal point. Often you might want to place a statue, a seat, some eye-catching flowers or a plant with bold foliage to act as an eye-catcher, but be careful not to overdo it—you only need one focal point in any view.

Against a garden's backdrop of green, nothing draws the eye like a spot of bright colour—it is for this reason that landscape painters have always been fond of adding a touch of scarlet at the focal points of their compositions. But flowers soon fade and even bold foliage has its off-seasons—a permanent feature like this urn on its pedestal is easier to plan for. It draws the eye by its very artificiality, its crisp form remaining all year. If you wanted to add a touch of colour, it would be easy enough to fill the urn with flowers, changing them as the seasons come and go.

ABOVE: Here is an interesting concept—two focal points. The enclosed garden is arranged symmetrically around the circular hedge, but the eye is drawn beyond it to the blue spruce framed in the arch, which in turn is the focus of the garden room beyond. A well-head can make a charming centre-piece for a formal garden like this and it doesn't have to be a well. A small, raised circular pond housing a goldfish or three would work just as nicely.

BELOW: When garden designers talk of 'vistas' this is exactly the sort of thing they mean. The eye travels along the manicured lawn, between the flanking trees, to come to rest on a distant focal point—a sundial. Its drawing power is enhanced, for the moment anyway, by the splash of autumn foliage and the sharp white of *Nerine flexuosa alba*. You could replace the sundial with a statue or dove-cote if you wanted.

GARDEN STYLES

'Style' can be a frightening concept. It suggests that if you break certain strict rules you will end up with a mess. Yet this is not so: the various styles of gardening are not so rigid as that and you can have a great deal of freedom in interpreting them. A cottage garden might contain 'formal' elements such as topiary or statues; a formal garden might contain casually mixed plantings of old-fashioned 'cottage garden' flowers—it is a matter of the mood you want to create.

Its starkly geometrical shape and the fine work of its stone surround make this pool a classic example of a very formal design. Yet the overall effect is of romance, especially when the rhododendrons bloom in spring. The pool itself is filled with water lilies and the shrubs have been allowed to grow almost wild, making the pool seem like a relic of some long-forgotten civilisation, lost in a wilderness of flowers.

FORMAL GARDENS

A formal design may be perfectly symmetrical and make much use of straight lines, circles and other geometrical shapes, or it may not, though there will always be a sense of careful balance.

In a formal garden you will find immaculately trimmed lawn, carefully pruned shrubs and hedges, trees arranged in avenues or evenly spaced shrubs and flowers carefully grouped in matching colours. The formal style is especially suited to the gardens of old houses, those planned for a lifestyle less casual than ours. Often if you find old pictures of the original garden, you'll find that it was very formal in layout and planting, especially if the house itself was symmetrical in design. There's no need to re-create a Victorian design for a Victorian house. After all, a modern dinner party is no stiff, strait-laced affair; and a modern formal garden need not be artificial and pompous—soften its lines with flowers and abundant foliage.

LEFT: Dividing a formal garden into four, with some elegant feature at the centre, is a tradition as old as gardening—the *Book of Genesis* speaks of Eden as being divided by four rivers. Indian and Persian gardens often follow suit with four pools fed from a central fountain, bringing coolness in their hot climates. Here the idea is carried out on a modest scale, with four gravel paths converging on a statue. The four beds are outlined with clipped box and filled with *Vinca minor*. Japanese cherry trees canopy the whole setting with spring flowers.

CARING FOR THE GARDEN

While a formal garden does look best if it is beautifully maintained, it need not be a high-maintenance garden. If you keep your plantings simple and choose plants that don't need much care, much of the work is simply garden housework —trimming edges, raking leaves or pruning hedges.

ABOVE: Elizabethan gardens often featured 'knots', or planting beds adorned with intricate patterns made up of interlacing lines of dwarf plants with contrasting foliage. The plants were usually clipped to ensure the pattern remained distinct. Here is a modern example, set on the lawn like a picture on a wall, and carefully centred on the line of the steps. The main pattern is worked in bright green box and grey lavender. The stone frame sets it all off—and keeps the lawn from invading.

TYPES OF ESPALIERS

Belgian fence espalier

Horizontal cordon espalier

Triple vertical U-shape espalier

Fan-trained espalier

TRAINING AN ESPALIER

Training an espalier begins in the plant's youth, when you select the branches that will form its framework, removing all those that don't conform to the desired shape. Those you save are tied back to a trellis, and as the plant grows it is pruned to maintain the shape. As it matures the pattern will become less distinct than it looks in the diagrams. Fruit trees such as apples, pears and peaches, or camellias, mock-oranges, cotoneasters, calliandras or hibiscus are all suitable subjects for espaliers.

ABOVE: Formal doesn't always mean grand and imposing. This is almost a cottage garden with its simple flowers and the way the statue that terminates the vista down the path is framed only by some roses and a small arch. Yet its formality lies in its geometry—the paths are quite straight, they meet at right angles and their lines are underscored by the plantings. Notice too how rigid symmetry is ignored in the treatment of the lawn edges: brick trim on one side, simple clipping to a line on the other.

ABOVE: At first sight, this garden is a composition in straight lines, the clipped hedges seeming almost as massive and solid as the stone seat. Yet look more closely: the pavement is made up of irregular slabs of stone, the trees are allowed to grow untrimmed, the climbing rose showers its delicate flowers over all. Is this a formal garden or an informal one with touches of formality? As the yellow cypress grows, would you clip it into a column or allow it to spread naturally?

LEFT: Here we have ranunculi, Californian poppies, wallflowers and lavender—all old-fashioned cottage-garden flowers—but the way they are grouped in blocks of one colour planted around the centre-piece of an old well-head gives them a formal air. They aren't planted in strips, the lowest in front, the taller behind, the way the municipal gardeners do, as that tends to look a little too formal for most gardens. Their frame of rich green box sets off their bright colours and links them to the backdrop of mature trees. Though dwarf box is the classic shrub for low hedges to edge formal flower beds, you don't have to use it. Consider plants such as lavender, rosemary, the grey-leaved lavender cotton (*Santolina*), the dwarf pomegranate (*Punica granatum* 'Nana'), dwarf nandina or any one of a number of dwarf-growing junipers and cypresses. Another alternative is the small growing kurume azaleas, clipped immediately after bloom.

ABOVE: There are few better ways of adding a touch of formality than with standard shrubs—ordinary shrubs that have been trained to a single stem. You can place them in pairs on either side of a gate, use one as the centre of a bed or, as here, arrange them along a path. These are clipped box: for a more casual effect, you could substitute standard roses. Notice how the two bay trees framing the end of the path have been pruned into narrow columns. Upright-growing camellias such as 'Shiragiku' could do the job too.

CREATING A STANDARD

1 Select a plant with a prominent central stem and stake if needed.

2 Clip off the growing tip and lower branches, removing unwanted shoots as they appear.

3 Continue to pinch out the growing tips to form a well-rounded head.

WILD GARDENS

If the essence of the formal garden is displaying the gardener's art and skill, that of the wild garden is concealing it so that everything looks as though it grew that way naturally.

Its most extreme form is the wild garden where only plants native to the area are grown, so that the garden appears as if the house was simply dropped in from a helicopter. Alternatively, you can use garden plants from anywhere in the world, planting trees and shrubs in informal, irregular groups, under-planting with groundcovers, but importantly, avoiding the horticultural zoo. Take a look at a truly wild landscape anywhere in the world, and you'll see that nature paints with quite a limited palette—just a few species, but each in large numbers. That needn't be as limiting as it sounds as most desirable species come in a number of varieties.

LEFT: In a subtropical garden, a simple path winds its way though the lush foliage. None of the plants is at all exotic, at least to warm-climate gardeners, and there are few flowers. The jungle effect comes from the closeness of the planting and the way the ferns and busy lizzies are allowed to come up wherever they please. The garden is much smaller than it looks, the illusion of size coming from the way the end of the path is unseen and the foliage is arranged—bold in the foreground, smaller and finer beyond. Both are techniques copied from Japanese gardens.

BOTTOM LEFT: Here plants from all over the temperate zones are brought together in a picture that Nature could never have planted. Yet it looks as though she might have, and that is tribute to the gardener's skill. The tidy-minded might object that it is high time the perennials had their dying leaves and spent flowers trimmed back but leaving them be only increases the natural effect. If you allow flowers to set and shed their seeds, there is a chance that they will 'go wild' and it is always such a delight to find a choice flower growing where it planted itself like a wildflower.

If you are making a garden on a site carved out from bushland, a wild garden can be a very sensible style to follow: the foundation is already there in the form of established trees and all you need to do is replace the other plants, shrubs and groundcovers that were destroyed in the inevitable disruption caused by building. After that, your main task is to keep the weeds from invading, something that mulching can greatly assist.

OPPOSITE: A hillside almost calls out for a wild garden, with paths zigzagging down and up again, revealing new views at every turn. Dispose your trees to give patterns of dappled sunshine and shade, add shrubs to break the view of one part of the path from another, and spread groundcovers to hold the slope against erosion. This garden shows a subtle detail—none of the plants is stiff and upright in habit, revealing their undersides from below: all arch and spread in graceful lines that echo the land itself.

VINES IN GARDENS

While vines are often thought of as simply functional plants—to be used to cover unsightly fences and structures with greenery and flowers, or to turn the bare structure of a pergola into a shady roof—they can do much more than that.

Vines such as wisteria, clematis, jasmine and climbing roses can festoon not only the house itself but trees and shrubs with flowers. Flowers are not their only charm; some have attractive leaves, other vines such as ivy make excellent groundcovers, while some, notably the grape, provide fruit as well. Vines come in two main types. There are those few, such as ivy, Virginia creeper and the Chinese trumpet vine (*Campsis*) that can cling to a wall or fence without assistance; others are designed to twine around branches or a trellis or to grip them with tendrils. Wisteria and the various jasmines are twiners; the grape and passionfruit are classic examples of vines with tendrils.

ABOVE: A climbing rose has grown to the top of this wall to hang sprays of flowers over into the picture. Below it, the English rose 'Shropshire Lass', a tall-growing shrub rose, masks the wall, not needing to be supported by it. In front grows feverfew (*Chrysanthemum parthenifolium*), an old-fashioned cottage flower. Officially perennial, it often flowers itself to death in a single summer, leaving a host of seedlings for next year. Its foliage is aromatic.
LEFT: Wisteria must rank with climbing roses as the best loved and most romantic of all climbing plants. It is a woody vine of immense vigour, though fortunately it is amenable to pruning. Here the Chinese wisteria, *Wisteria sinensis*, drapes its scented blossoms over a gum tree. The Japanese wisteria, *W. floribunda*, bears longer trails of flowers a couple of weeks later. Both are available in either mauve or white.

ABOVE: Though it has no flowers worth mentioning, Virginia creeper (*Parthenocissus*) is an old favourite for covering fences and other eyesores because it clings by itself without the need for a trellis. Before the leaves fall in autumn, they blaze in brilliant colours of red and orange. Here the creeper softens the lines of a brick wall, making a backdrop to tree trunks and a clump of bamboo. The white flowers in front are freeway daisies (*Osteospermum eklonis*) which flower from spring to autumn. Appropriately for its position on the street side of the wall, this is an easy-care planting.

TRAINING A VINE

1 Most vines tend to grow up a wall resulting in thicker growth at the top and bare branches below. By spreading out the shoots of a young vine this can be prevented.

2 Train some of the branches to grow out horizontally. Small shoots will grow from these horizontal branches resulting in a denser, more even coverage of leaves.

ROMANTIC GARDENS

It's hard to clearly define the one quality that makes a garden romantic. It can be the location—a tiny city garden shaded by a single tree with a seat where you can sit and listen to a splashing fountain can be romantic, so can a tropical garden with palms silvered by the moonlight; or it can be a garden where the plants themselves create the mood, like a beautiful rose garden. Whatever it is, the gardens on the next four pages have one thing in common—a profusion of flowers in gentle colours. There are no sharp contrasts here, no scarlets and oranges, and no intrusions of ugly buildings and structures on the view.

Romantic gardens, essentially, are not designed to receive a crowd of people even though they may be quite large. A sense of seclusion is a part of their charm: the romantic garden is a place set apart from the world.

ABOVE: When you trust as much ground as this to a single perennial flower, it had better offer something to look at when the blossoms are over. Columbines are ideal: their greyish leaves are beautifully cut and handsome all summer. These are the old-fashioned *Aquilegia vulgaris*, also known as 'granny's bonnets'. The long-spurred hybrids are even more graceful and offer a wider range of colour than *A. vulgaris* does, but their leaves are not so handsome and they don't come up from self-sown seed nearly as freely, an important quality in columbines. (None is very long-lived.) Temperate to cool climates suit them best.
LEFT: There are few sights more romantic than an orchard in spring, its delicate blossoms offering delight for the moment and the promise of fruit to come. Here a half-dozen young apple trees rise from a carpet of bluebells. A tiny rock-rimmed stream adds its music and a dozen white tulips complete the picture.

LEFT: Spring bulbs never look happier than when 'naturalised' in grass among trees. The trick is to have them looking as though they came up by themselves—no straight lines or circular plantings. You can achieve a similar effect by taking a handful of bulbs and scattering them the way children do marbles. Plant the bulbs where they fall. The daffodils and 'Heavenly Blue' grape hyacinths we see here are happiest in cool climates. Where winters are mild you could use freesias, sparaxis or even small spring-blooming gladioli such as *Gladiolus blandus* or *G. cardinalis*.

In a tropical or subtropical climate, you could create a spectacular show by naturalising hippeastrums (amaryllis), especially the new Dutch hybrids which come in much subtler colours than the old-fashioned varieties. They aren't cheap, but you can build up a collection by saving their seed and growing it. Seedlings come up quickly and will flower in their third spring.

SPRING BULBS

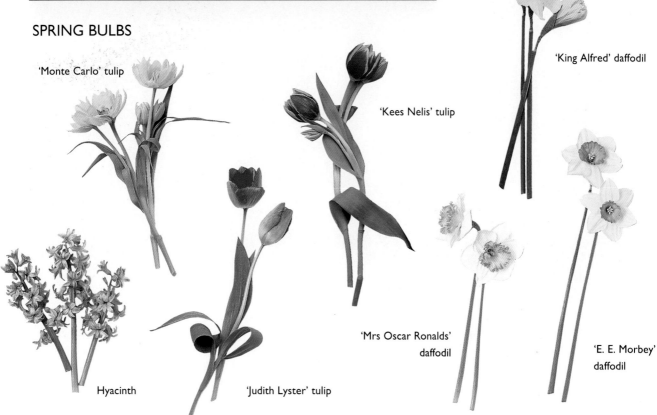

'King Alfred' daffodil

'Monte Carlo' tulip

'Kees Nelis' tulip

'Mrs Oscar Ronalds' daffodil

'E. E. Morbey' daffodil

Hyacinth

'Judith Lyster' tulip

An enclosed garden where you can retreat unobserved is not only useful for dalliance but it can be a great place to escape from the children and the television. No need for walls and a locked gate: all you need to do is to arrange plantings of sufficient height that your secret garden is private, as has been done in this charming corner with its central birdbath. Nor do you need to keep the secret too closely: here a gap in the high hedges provides tantalizing glimpses for the outsider.

ABOVE: Viburnums, forget-me-nots and bluebells make a quiet corner among the pale green leaves of spring. Would the picture be as charming without the little figure that has taken up residence in the birdbath? Come summer, she will have a setting of Mexican daisies (*Erigeron mucronatus*) which bear myriads of small white and soft pink flowers.

BELOW LEFT: The fairy-tale beauty of this garden comes as much from the soft colour scheme of white, pale pink and blue as from the way the flowers are allowed to grow seemingly as they will,

even in the crevices between the paving stones. Imagine a single scarlet tulip added to the picture—the spell would be broken. The white flowers in the little pond (left foreground) are *Aponogeton distachyos*, the water hawthorn, which derives its common name from its scent.

BELOW RIGHT: There's always a touch of romance in an overgrown garden. This garden is a lovely example: the paving stones are almost hidden by lowly foliage, and on all sides flowers (columbines, viburnums, *Iris japonica*) grow freely.

COTTAGE GARDENS

Unlike the formal garden which had its origins in palaces and grand country houses, the cottage garden originated in the gardens of the ordinary people with little money and far less leisure time.

Cottage gardens were small and flowers had to share the space with vegetables and herbs. Unlike the flowers in a formal garden, cottage flowers were enjoyed and loved for themselves, not as mere 'plant material'. The favourite flowers were those easy-to-grow ones that today we call 'old-fashioned'. They were easy to propagate too, and many a cottage garden was stocked with plants that originated as cuttings passed over the fence by a friend. The result was a happy mixture of flowers and other plants, mixed and matched as the gardener's fancy suggested, without too much thought of careful colour schemes and formal design. That is the essence of this style of garden—it is one for the true flower lover, and it can be a great deal of fun as well.

LEFT: It is always charming to allow flowers to spill over a fence onto the street to delight passers-by—and perhaps to encourage them to stop for a few minute's conversation. However, don't be tempted to use prickly plants such as roses or bougainvillea which have thorns that may injure passers-by. Here chrysanthemums sprawl over the fence above a groundcover of Mexican daisies. Potted chrysanthemums are available in bloom all year and the season for garden-grown ones is autumn.

TROPICAL CLIMATES

While traditional cottage flowers are the perennials and annuals of temperate climates, there is no reason why the style cannot be adapted to subtropical climates, using some of the perennial flowers and bulbs such as heliconias, daylilies, hippeastrums, cannas, crinums, even orchids, together with the many warm-climate annuals.

LEFT: When planning a cottage garden there is no need to confine yourself to 'old-fashioned' flowers. Grow your favourites and arrange them so that each sets off its neighbours—colours in contrast and harmony, rounded flowers set off by spiky ones or annuals mixed with perennials. In this garden, blue and pink larkspurs and blood-red Flanders poppies grow together in a late-spring display that isn't quite as artless as it looks—they have been chosen to contrast in shape as well as colour, the tall spikes of the larkspurs setting off the round cups of the poppies. Both are annuals and the permanent framework of the planting is provided by roses which will reach their peak bloom as their companions begin to fade.

BELOW: Annuals need not be planted in massed beds on their own, municipal-garden style. They can be just as effective when small groups are tucked in among other plants—a dozen here, a half dozen there. Here are four old-fashioned favourites: pansies (top left); petunias (top right); cosmos, alias the Mexican aster (bottom left); and sweet peas (bottom right). All of these flowers are suited to almost any climate.

PLANNING A COTTAGE GARDEN

Flowers en masse can be pretty shapeless so it is wise to start with a good, bold plan. The old cottagers recognised this so they made their paths straight and their lines bold. We should do the same, underscoring the paths by edging the beds with a single low-growing plant and arranging to give them flattering backgrounds of hedges, trees or flowery shrubs.

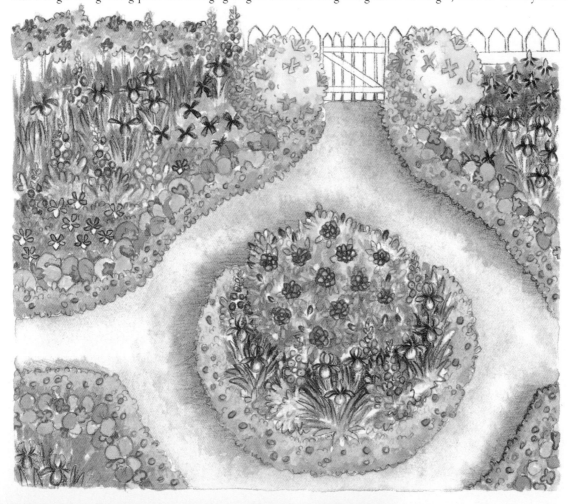

LEFT: Here's the versatile Mexican daisy (*Erigeron mucronatus*) again, this time edging a bright planting of cream and gold Californian poppies, and mauve and magenta perennial wallflowers (*Cheiranthus mutabilis*). The ordinary biennial wallflowers with their gold-to-russet colour range are cottage garden favourites too. The perennial wallflower is a really useful plant for its scent and extremely long season of bloom, from autumn through a mild winter until late spring. The plant is bushy in growth, so to keep it compact and long lived you need to harden your heart and cut it back rather severely when the flowers begin to deteriorate with the onset of hot weather.

LEFT: It is an old maxim that when you are mixing flowers, you shouldn't just plant one or two of each kind but plant them in generous groups. That way the different colours form a pattern rather than a series of multi-coloured spots. But there is no need to have your groups all the same size— a small group of a large, eye-catching flower can balance a larger planting of something less assertive. In this picture, a few tall double poppies and a rose bush are set off by an extensive group of white evening primroses and a smaller clump of the white gladiolus, 'The Bride'. The whole effect is tied together by an edging of vivid blue catmint which adds scent and grey-green foliage.

ABOVE: This cottage garden displays a beautifully cool colour scheme of blue and white flowers—*Campanula persicifolia*, delphiniums and Mexican daisies—and grey foliage—lavender, buddleias and *Lychnis coronaria*. The magenta flowers of the lychnis don't spoil the basic scheme; rather they spice it up just enough to keep it from looking bland and contrived. If you prefer the blue and white scheme, there is also a white-flowered version available.

ABOVE: Roses are almost indispensable to the cottage style and mixing them with other flowers has the advantage of hiding their thorny legs. Here the floribunda, 'Orange Triumph', (despite its name, it is actually scarlet) lines one side of the path, an assortment of climbing roses trained on tall stakes, the other. Notice how the cushions of mauve campanulas and the grassy leaves of daylilies soften and balance the severely straight line of the garden path.

FRAGRANT GARDENS

Part of the magic of a garden is its scents. There is the subtle scent of freshly mown grass and of the very earth itself after the rain. Then there are the more obvious scents of flowers. Some, such as jasmine, wisteria or daphne, can't be missed; they are wafted on the air for metres around. Others, such as afternoon roses or mollis azaleas, have to be sought by bending your nose to the flower, and then there are some flowers that only offer their scent at certain times of day, as tobacco flowers and many orchids do, so that if you make their acquaintance at the wrong time you may forever think of them as scentless.

There are many plants whose scent is in their leaves, to be released only after a shower of rain or when you brush against them or crush them. Lavender, rosemary, cistus, thyme and scented geraniums offer delight for a much longer season than flowers do, and no garden should be without some.

The usual rule that you shouldn't plant so close to a path that walking will be interfered with can be suspended in the case of lavender, here just coming into bloom. If you didn't brush it as you walked past, you'd miss out on the pleasure of its perfume, which clings subtly to your clothes for some time. Its scent always seems to harmonise with roses—the other main flower in the picture—but you don't want to brush against their thorny stems. Place them within smelling distance but not too close!

TOP: Many of the viburnums offer a truly delicious fragrance, but not the one that features so strongly here—the snowball tree or guelder rose (*Viburnum opulus* 'Sterile'). Its attraction is its extraordinary display of creamy-white flowers. Yet there is scent abounding in this garden—roses, catmint and Japanese wisteria.

BOTTOM: The high season of this garden is spring, when the green euphorbias on the left set off the pale pink magnolia on the right. The summer picture of varied greens with just a few touches of colour is lovely too—and it has the added dimension of scent from the leaves of the rosemary and the cistus on its left.

ABOVE: Wisteria is such a classic vine for clothing walls and pergolas that it can be a surprise to see it grown as a shrub. (You can keep it that way by training the young plants on a stake and then cutting back the new growths as they grow in summer.

Eventually the branches become self-supporting.) A garden devoted almost entirely to wisteria is a rare sight in the West, though an old tradition in China and Japan. The scent of a wisteria garden can be overwhelming, yet it is one of those scents that never cloys.

LEFT: The blending of the green and purple-leaved basil creates an interesting effect though the full joy of the planting cannot be captured by the camera. It is the truly beautiful scent of the basil leaves, each kind subtly different but all refreshing and delightful. Oddly enough, most insects hate it, and it is said that if you plant basil around any place intended for outdoor dining neither flies nor mosquitoes will bother you.

OPPOSITE: All the magnolias are scented, with a soft, sweet fragrance though the strongest and sweetest is probably the summer-blooming evergreen *Magnolia grandiflora*, a magnificent tree for large gardens. The spring flowering deciduous magnolias are fragrant also: this is the best known of them, *M. soulangiana*, a smallish tree for temperate and cool climates.

GREEN GARDENS

Green is the colour for the busy gardener. It takes a lot of work to maintain a display of flowers all year, arranging for each star performer to take over as the one before retires, but leaves are on stage all year.

Even in a cool-climate winter when the deciduous trees and shrubs stand bare and the herbaceous perennials have retired underground, there are plenty of evergreens to keep the green theme alive. When you cultivate an eye for green, it is wonderful how many different shades there are: from emerald, olive, silvery and greyish greens to the almost yellow tones of the young leaves of deciduous trees in spring. And there are the uncommon but surprisingly many green flowers. Add to that the variety of shapes and sizes that leaves offer, and you have as rich a palette as any garden artist could ask for. There is no need to worry about subtlety in deploying it—that you have limited yourself to shades of the one colour guarantees that.

LEFT: Green flowers are not as showy as the flowers of, say, irises—but there are surprising numbers of them. Few actually have green petals: most make their display with green sepals or from green bracts that give importance to otherwise insignificant flowers. Among these are the green euphorbias, of which this one, the late-spring blooming *Euphorbia wulfenii*, is perhaps the best known. You may find it listed as *E. characias* subspecies *wulfenii*: the exact classification of the several hundred species of *Euphorbia* is a headache for botanists. Like most green flowers, it remains in beauty for a long time.

GREEN GARDENING

A green garden need not be a bland or flowerless one. There are greens of every intensity, from the palest to almost black. The colour of the leaf is influenced by its texture: the exact same shade will look subtly different if the surface is matt or if it's glossy. A green garden gives you scope to experiment with contrasts. Think, for instance, of the boldly cut leaves of acanthus set against a wall clad in a small-leaved ivy, or of the spiky leaves of irises contrasted with the round ones of nasturtiums. And don't forget that the colours of paving, fences and the house will play a part in the overall effect too.

ABOVE: The spring display of bulbs and annuals is over and only a few forget-me-nots remain to spangle the varied greens of late spring with pale blue. As summer advances, the leaves will deepen to a richer, more uniform green; come autumn the picture will change again as they assume their autumn dress of gold and scarlet.

BELOW: With colour limited to green, shape and form assume a new importance. Notice how the fine long leaves of the mondo grass edging contrast with the broad leaves of the liquidambar and the small round ones of the box, each catching and reflecting the light in its own way.

SHADY GARDENS

Most gardens go through a change in character as they grow up. Unless you have been lucky enough to inherit trees that were there before the house was built, your new garden will be essentially a sunny one. Over time your trees grow up, and the garden slowly transforms itself into a shaded one. If you take over an established garden, thinning the trees is often the first step in renovating it, though don't just lop your shady trees—they'll only grow back bushier. Instead, thin out their branches, transforming the solid canopy into a lacy one, and your full shade into dappled shade.

There are many plants that enjoy the shade and they include some of the loveliest of all: camellias, rhododendrons, violets, anthuriums, orchids, bromeliads, and the many tropical lilies that grow in hot climates.

ABOVE: Evergreen azaleas are unrivalled among shade-loving shrubs for sheer prodigality of flower—at the height of their spring season you can hardly see a leaf. Lime-free soil and cool winters (with no frost) suit the plants best.

RIGHT: The silver birch (*Betula pendula*) is one of the best trees for the suburban garden—it grows fast but not too large, is well-suited to plantings in small groups and never casts too dense a shade. Its silver trunks and fresh green leaves almost cry out for cool colours in the flowers planted at its feet: white and soft pinks, as pictured, or soft pinks and blues. Birches are trees for cool- to cold-winter climates,

but in the subtropics you could re-create this picture with one of the several white-trunked, smaller growing eucalypts.

OPPOSITE: A large tree can create a pool of shade in an otherwise sunny garden, and it doesn't have to be very large to give you the opportunity of playing with shade-loving plants. Here a variegated holly shelters a rhododendron, one of the new compact-growing hybrids derived from the Japanese *Rhododendron yakushimanum*. The lustrous darkness of its leaves is more than matched by that of the black mondo grass, perhaps the darkest leaved of all garden plants. Most rhododendrons are lovers of cool climates and lime-free soil.

ORIENTAL GARDENS

In all Oriental gardens, immaculate maintenance is called for: no fallen leaves, no gravel that isn't raked over daily and definitely no weeds! Azaleas are shaped to harmonise with the rocks and pines are thinned to expose their gnarled, ancient-looking branches. (Those seemingly natural trees are often as carefully disciplined as any topiary.) Horticultural interest is not the focal point. There might be flowers in season such as azaleas, wisteria, irises or cherry blossoms, or there might be a flash of coloured leaves in autumn, but the important elements are rocks, water and trees, arranged to give the feeling that you are sitting by a mountain stream. If the garden is too tiny for a real stream, it can be simulated by one with rocks and raked white gravel.

For all its apparent naturalness, the Oriental style garden, especially the Japanese, is an austere one: simplicity is everything.

ABOVE: This garden evokes a mixture of Asian styles with its simple paving, lush semitropical planting, and its accessories—a Balinese sculpture and a Japanese lantern. The lantern is of the kind the Japanese call a 'snow-viewing' lantern (it is designed to allow the snow to drift between its legs rather than pile up all over it) but it looks quite at home with the sculpture.

LEFT: Here is a beautiful and successful example of translating the Japanese temple garden into a Western idiom. In Japan, this gate would be made of bamboo rather than wrought iron, but it is authentic in its proportions, in the way it allows us to see into the garden beyond, and in the little roof (of tea tree rather than Japanese thatch) which turns it into a kind of arch. The way the figure of the Buddha is framed by the branches of the white camellia is a lovely touch. The camellia is the Australian-raised 'Polar Bear' and the trees are not Japanese pines but gums, yet the style of the garden is as convincingly Japanese as anyone could desire.

ABOVE: Here we see a fine old water basin, carved in the shape of a Chinese coin and placed at the entrance to the garden so you can purify your fingers and thoughts before proceeding further. The arrangement of bamboo water pipes is traditional and beautifully done, but you could omit it if you wanted to. The lantern serves to light the basin should you visit the garden by night, and the whole is framed by the dwarf azalea (to be admired as you bend down to the water) and the camellia.

BELOW: This is not an overtly Oriental garden; there are no goldfish ponds and pagodas here. Yet in composing the picture with the simplest of means, the designer has followed Oriental precepts. A curving path, its stones arranged as artfully as the squares of gold leaf on a Japanese screen, massed azaleas and camellias and an edging of mondo grass all combine to create a sense of perfect, tranquil harmony which Japanese gardeners regard as the signature of a true artist.

ROSE GARDENS

Part of the attraction of the rose is the variety it offers, and few rose-lovers can resist collecting as many different cultivars as possible.

While it is possible to specialise in a particular flower without unbalancing the garden, the secret is to create a green framework that looks good even without the flowers. That will give you something to admire in the off season; and in full season, the green backdrop will flatter your flowers. To do this, place trees and evergreen shrubs to form the garden 'walls', arranging the rose beds within them. Separate the beds with paths to allow you to escort admiring visitors.

This style is suited to formal gardens but roses also lend themselves to cottage gardens. Here they are not grown on their own but mixed with other flowers. Blue flowers such as irises and delphiniums always look fabulous as they perfectly complement any of the vast range of rose colours but you can mix and match as you want.

All roses are shrubs to the botanist, but gardeners use the term 'shrub roses' to describe varieties that grow taller, bushier and more gracefully than the large and cluster-flowered bedding roses, whose stiffly upright branches rarely look elegant. The beauty of the individual flowers of the shrub roses is less important than the prodigious freedom with which they bear them. Here are three favourites in full late-spring flight: the deep pink 'Elmshorn', the medium-pink, single-flowered 'Ballerina' and the deliciously fragrant, almost-white 'Penelope'.

TOP LEFT: Yellow roses tend to need more care than those of other colours, especially in humid-summer climates where the black-spot fungus is troublesome. This cluster-flowered bush, 'Golden Gloves', has a nice fragrance and a good reputation for health. BOTTOM LEFT: The popular 'Class Act' has large white flowers warmed by cream. TOP RIGHT: 'Sweet Inspiration' is notable for its soft colouring, beautiful flower shape and great freedom of bloom. It is a compact bush, usually around a metre tall and wide. BOTTOM RIGHT: 'Double Delight' is a popular choice for its beautiful flower shape, its unique colour and superb fragrance. It is best enjoyed in the vase rather than in the garden as the bush is gawky in habit with undistinguished foliage.

PRUNING
COTTAGE GARDEN ROSES

The rose is one of the few shrubby plants that is conventionally pruned every year. How you prune your roses has a big influence on how your bushes will look. Regular pruning makes any shrubby plant look more formal; the harder you prune the more pronounced this effect will be. In a cottage garden you don't need to prune so hard. If you cut your bushes down half-way you'll be rewarded by exhibition-standard flowers but if you prune lightly, only cutting out dead branches and then shortening the rest by no more than a third, you'll get larger, more natural-looking plants plus a great abundance of flowers. Nor do you have to prune each winter: one often finds unpruned roses in old gardens, and they are usually enormous and smothered in flowers.

TYPES OF ROSES

Miniature roses grow to only 30 cm or less, with leaves and flowers in perfect proportion.

Growing from 1.5 m tall, old-fashioned or heritage roses offer rich colours and fragrance.

Climbing roses grow from 2.5 to 5 m in height and width. They may bear their flowers singly or in clusters.

Wild roses are mostly big, arching shrubs, growing to 2 m or more in height and width. They bloom in spring; many have attractive fruit (hips) in autumn.

Bush roses are classed as large or cluster flowered. They vary in height—1.2 m is about average.

LEFT: Climbing roses are among the most versatile plants in gardening, bringing colour and sweet scent even to gardens where roses otherwise don't appear. Their great vigour allows them to compete for light and nourishment better than bush roses can, so you can plant other plants, even shrubs, close to their feet. Just remember that they need to be able to grow up into the sunshine. This climbing rose is 'Wedding Day', with myriads of little five-petalled flowers that waft delightful fragrance in their late-spring season. Its leaves are glossy and attractive. The only pruning it needs is for the oldest, worn-out branches to be cut out in winter.

MIXED PLANTING

When mixing and matching roses with other flowers don't plant a bed full of roses and then try to squeeze the other flowers in between. This only encourages rose diseases which flourish best when the leaves are deprived of light and fresh air. Plant the roses in small groups, allowing the usual metre or so between them and then space your groups at least two metres apart. Don't forget to allow space in front for low-growing flowers to mask the roses' bad legs.

RIGHT: The traditional scheme of planting roses in a formal arrangement of beds of their own has much to commend it. Not only are the bushes placed where they can get plenty of sun and air but it also makes it easier to give them regular attention by way of mulching, spraying, grooming and pruning. The artificial appearance of roses set in bare earth is greatly improved by edging the beds with low foliage to mask the bushes' thorny stems. In this picture, pinks do the job but you could use dwarf box, lavender or even parsley. Here the roses are brilliantly fitted into the overall design by the simple expedient of confining them to the raised terrace to create two contrasting but linked garden 'rooms'.

CAMELLIA GARDENS

Camellias are often compared with roses and while they do have some similarities, they play a very different role in the garden. The camellia is not a plant for flower beds: it is a substantial shrub, head high or more, and is ideally suited to playing a starring role in the garden's basic, permanent framework.

There are thousands of varieties to choose from, ranging in shades from white and pink to red. *Camellia japonica*, the best known species, is a compact, shapely grower, well-suited to the formal style of gardening. Camellias are naturally woodland plants and also lend themselves beautifully to the wild, woodland style, where they can be disposed in informal, natural-looking groups beneath a canopy of trees. Here you can mix your japonicas with any of the other species and their cultivars and hybrids: *C. sasanqua*, *reticulata*, *lutchuensis*, *rosaeflora* and others. Most are less formal in habit, and some, like *C. lutchuensis*, offer delicious fragrance.

ABOVE: This *Camellia sasanqua* is being grown as an informal espalier. Its name, 'Mine-no-yuki', appropriately means 'snow on the mountain'. With its fairly rapid, graceful growth, glossy evergreen leaves and abundant autumn bloom, the *Camellia sasanqua* ranks very high among desirable shrubs for temperate climates. The flowers are scented and the plants are more tolerant of full sunshine than most camellias.

LEFT: Left to itself, *Camellia sasanqua* grows into a small tree, though it may take thirty years or so. Like most camellias it can easily be kept at almost any size you like by regular pruning. This camellia, 'Plantation Pink', is about ten years old and has been shaped by removing the lower branches to expose its pale grey trunk and by regular shortening back of the branches.

LEFT: Named for the Californian nurseryman who created it, Guilio Nuccio, this japonica is often called the finest camellia in the world. It is admired for the huge size of its flowers, as big as saucers, and for its long blooming season from early winter until well into spring. This camellia has a brilliant coral-red colour which colour film rarely captures in its full beauty. It is a slow-growing, shapely shrub. Like all camellias, it prefers a temperate climate with humid summers, perfectly drained, lime-free soil, and a position sheltered from hot sun and drying wind. Camellias love being mulched with old manure or compost.

RIGHT: Flowers with striped and variegated petals either appeal or they do not, but if you like them—and many gardeners adore them—*Camellia japonica* offers the widest selection of any flower. They are best placed where you can admire them in close-up: at a distance the effect can be restless. The camellia pictured is 'Betty Foy Sanders'. Don't be at all surprised to find it producing the odd branch with flowers in solid pink, a habit called 'sporting' and one of which camellias are very fond. It is not uncommon to find an old camellia tree bearing flowers of two or three different colours.

LEFT: *Camellia japonica* is the most widely grown camellia, a slow-growing shrub of compact habit, very handsome foliage and splendid flowers in every shade from white to deep red. The white varieties such as this one, 'Silver Chalice', are especially effective in the garden, the deep glossy green of the leaves making their intense whiteness seem even more perfect. White and pale pink camellias need to be carefully placed where they won't be touched by the early morning sun, which will boil the frost or dew off the flowers and cook them to a most unappealing dirty brown. A little sun later in the day will do them no harm.

TROPICAL GARDENS

While tropical and subtropical gardens mature quickly because of the heat, they can also be hard work as the constant warmth means that everything grows fast and furiously. A tropical garden can be kept formal—tightly clipped and under control, or it can be wildly informal. It can be a study in different greens, or it can be the proverbial riot of colour, with the strong colours of cannas, hibiscus, frangipani, oleanders and bougainvillea.

When planning a tropical garden all the usual considerations apply—you still need to consider privacy, how to cover the 'floor' of the garden, how to provide a safe access to the house and importantly, how to provide shade. Trees and pergolas with creepers are as useful here as elsewhere though don't forget that the tropical sun is higher at noon, no matter what the season, so you need to place trees where their branches will be directly overhead.

ABOVE: While palm groves may be synonymous with tropical gardening, here is an unusual variation on the theme—a tree-fern grove. Naturally denizens of the sheltered rainforest, some tree ferns will take happily to growing in the open, though they do need shelter from drying summer winds. These cyatheas look splendid rising from the green carpet of grass.

LEFT: One of the surprises that awaits the visitor to the tropics is the sight of indoor plants flourishing mightily in the garden. Here a collection of crotons display their multi-coloured leaves at the foot of a palm. The croton (*Codiaeum variegatum*) is an evergreen (or should that be ever-colourful?) shrub, sturdy enough to be used for hedges. It loves rich soil and regular watering, and grows well in sun or shade. There are many named varieties, differing in the shape and colour of the leaves.

It isn't at all difficult to re-create your own tropical rainforest in the garden: plant some trees—whatever takes your fancy—and fill in beneath them with an assortment of shrubs and lower growing plants. As the trees grow up, you can plant climbers to grow up into them, and maybe adorn their branches with epiphytic orchids.

Creating a rainforest is much the same thing as creating a temperate-climate wild garden, only your palette of plants is richer and the rainforest doesn't bloom all at once in spring the way a temperate forest does. Rather, it scatters a few flowers at a time over a background of varied foliage.

ABOVE: Cymbidiums are among the few orchids that grow on handsome plants. In China, where several of the parent species originate, their long, gracefully arching leaves are thought as attractive a feature as the flowers themselves. In the mild-winter climates where they can live permanently out of doors, they can make as attractive a massed display as, say, daylilies do. These are grown in pots, the pots themselves being half-buried in mulch both to hide them and to provide even moisture and coolness to the orchid roots. The main cymbidium season is spring though it is a very long one.

LEFT: The hibiscus occupies the same place in tropical gardens that the rose does in temperate ones—and some people would say it is the better plant, as its growth and evergreen foliage are much more handsome. There are hundreds of varieties, ranging from the 'Hawaiian hybrids' with dinner-plate sized flowers on rose bush-sized shrubs to shrubs that grow well over head high and equally wide. Just about every colour is available. This is 'Wilder's White', one of the tallest. Indeed it is tall enough that by removing its lower branches you can transform it into a small tree. The smaller growing types are first-rate shrubs for growing in tubs. Keep them compact and in proportion by pruning in spring just as growth is beginning.

ORCHIDS

If there is anything that makes a visitor to the tropics jealous, it is the sight of orchids growing in the garden. Yet orchids are not exclusively tropical and there are many beauties that can be grown outside where heavy frost does not occur. While their way of life usually means they have to be grown in pots or hanging baskets, a collection of potted plants can be a pleasing garden feature in its own right. We see some orchids on these two pages but you may like to substitute pots of orchids for the potted plants scattered through the gardens elsewhere in this book.

TOP LEFT: The miniature-flowered cymbidiums have become very popular in recent years: they have a certain elegance that many of their larger flowered cousins lack, and many are sweetly fragrant. Their flower spikes often arch down below the leaves which makes them one of the best of all flowers for growing in hanging baskets. Like all orchids, the important thing is not to overwater them in winter. Dormant orchid roots can cope with being cold, but they can't cope with being wet as well. It is, however, difficult to overwater orchids in hot weather.

MIDDLE LEFT: Cattleyas are perhaps the most glamorous and sought-after orchids, and they have two seasons of bloom— some flower in autumn, others in spring. They are usually grown in pots in greenhouses, but a surprising number will flourish out of doors in a warm-temperate climate and there you can grow them as they do naturally, attached to the branches of a tree. Choose one with rough bark, like a casuarina or bottlebrush, unpot the orchid and tie it in place, packing some sphagnum moss around its roots. Water and fertilise the orchid regularly in summer.

BOTTOM LEFT: This Cooktown orchid (*Dendrobium bigibbum*) is the state flower of Queensland, Australia. (Its own leaves are rather dull: those pictured are croton leaves.) This orchid has a reputation for being tricky to grow but happily it has been the parent of some very beautiful and less temperamental hybrids for subtropical gardens. These are grown in much the same way as cattleyas are. Most orchids, including this one, are becoming very rare as wild flowers and it is illegal to take them from the bush. Always buy your own from a government-licensed grower.

WATER GARDENS

Some of the most beautiful gardens ever designed have been essentially water gardens, composed around pools, lakes and fountains. Even today, there is no lovelier focal point for a garden than water sparkling in the sunlight.

You can treat water formally, in a pool of geometric shape with edges of cut stone or brick, or you can imitate a natural pool or stream. Either way, adorn the pool with beautiful water-dwelling plants such as water lilies, arums and Louisiana irises. A formal pool can be placed anywhere your design requires but a natural one must fit in with the shape of the land—remember that streams and ponds are found in hollows and low places. It will look silly half-way up a hill, and if you can't contrive a suitable hollow, then it is usually best to opt for a formal or semi-formal treatment, softening it with planting.

ABOVE: You don't have to have a pond to enjoy the wet-ground plants—you can create an artificial bog. It is easy to do: dig the soil away to a depth of half a metre or so, line the excavation with the same sort of plastic sheet you line a pond with, punch a hole or two at the lowest point and cover the base with a layer of stones to ensure the 'bog' doesn't become stagnant, then put the earth back. To keep everything wet, let the hose trickle on it as needed. There's no need for the bog to be round; here a long, narrow one suggests a little stream, with a bridge to complete the illusion.

OPPOSITE: A grand garden in the English manner, with lawns and borders of flowers leading down to a small lake which forms the focal point of the whole garden. The effect would be lost if it were entirely covered with water lilies; then you wouldn't see the glitter of sunlight on the water—just more leaves. The margins of the lake are lavishly planted with water-loving flowers: irises, arum lilies and bog primroses. Be careful with white arums in subtropical climates as they can easily take over wet ground and become pests. In Perth, Western Australia, they are prohibited for this reason.

BUILDING A POND

When building a pond heavy-duty plastic liners are cheap and easier to use than the traditional cement. Here's how to use one:

1 Mark out the shape on the ground using a hose, string and pegs.

2 Dig out the pond, sloping the sides at a 45 degree angle. A shelf about 35 cm wide can be left for marginal plants.

3 Lay the liner in the pond (placing a little sand under any pot-holes). Black plastic is best: blue looks like a swimming pool. Ensure all seams are watertight, and then hide the bottom with some river pebbles.

4 Ensure the liner covers all edges of the pond, and trim it to about 20 cm all round.

5 Place or cement stones or bricks around the edge to hide the plastic. Fill with water and stock with plants and fish.

5

ABOVE: Unless it is to be an outdoor aquarium sustained by pumps and filters and an owner who visits daily to feed the fish, a garden pool needs to be set up so it can become a self-sustaining environment. That means that you need to have fish to eat any mosquito larvae, and submerged and floating plants to keep the water charged with oxygen for them. Here, in a tropical pool, we see a floating cover of water lettuce, in nice balance with the clear areas of water: the ideal is to have half to two-thirds of the water surface open to the sunlight.

BELOW: This forest pool with goldfish looks as though it has always been here and the garden built around it. This is not the case: it is in fact built in concrete in the conventional way. The secrets of its success are two: first, the edges are masked with foliage so no cement is visible to strike a note of artificiality; and second, you can't see the fence which is only metres away, so densely is it planted out. As water lilies prefer the sun it is best to set a pond in full sunlight, but if you are prepared to forego them, a shaded pool can be a great success: the fish don't mind either way.

COUNTRY GARDENS

If the main problem of creating a suburban or city garden is creating privacy and accommodating your ideas to the space available, the country gardener has the opposite problem. Privacy is rarely an issue: here the task is to make use of all that space and to exploit the views out of the garden to the surrounding countryside. The best way to do this is to concentrate your intensively developed garden near the house, gradually leading the eye out through clumps of trees into the open country. This allows you to temper your ambitions to the time you have available for gardening.

One of the joys of country gardening is being able to make grand plans for sweeping vistas, great banks of trees and shrubs that grow too big to fit into a city garden. Think boldly—no intricate arrangements of one of this and two of that. Leave that to the city garden.

Perennial flowers naturally grow in meadows and they never look better than when you can plant them in generous, sweeping masses. Mixing them with herbs such as lavender and fennel is very much in the country-cottage tradition. Most herbs are drought resistant, an important factor to consider where summers are long and hot and water has to be doled out from tanks and dams.

ABOVE: A formal avenue of evenly spaced trees can turn a gravel track into the grandest of entrance drives. These are silver birches, fast-growing trees that give an effect of maturity in a few years. The back-up planting of assorted shrubs is something that avenue planters often neglect, but they are important. Not only do they keep the eye from straying sideways between the tree trunks, they help the appearance of the avenue when viewed from outside: all too often, it can look like the back view of a stage set. The statues between the trees give just a hint of the 'Grand Manner' but aren't so grand you'd be disappointed should the house not turn out to be a palace.

BIRD FEEDER

What country garden would be complete without the delight of watching native birds feeding. This bird feeder can be easily constructed from wood but ensure the roof overlaps the base to keep the seed dry.

LEFT: A touch of formality can be a great help in keeping a country garden from becoming shapeless but it needs to be a relaxed kind of formality. The casually shaped rosemary hedge and the lavender that surround the beds in the distance, strike a perfect balance between strictness and rustic informality. Separating the vegetable garden from the flower garden is an old-fashioned post and rail fence. They were traditionally painted white or cream so that horses could see them clearly and not stumble over them. This style of fence would also suit a cottage-style suburban garden. The wisteria, naturally a huge, rampaging vine, can be tailored to a restricted space or to a fence like this one by regular pruning. Prune in summer, cutting back the long, whippy shoots that arise soon after the flowers are over. Cut them back to three or four leaves as this encourages the short shoots that bear the flowers. Pruning in winter only encourages more growth and few flowers.

RIGHT: Where space is not at a premium, it can be tempting to make your beds big and wide. Be careful though: big can be spectacular, wide can be a bother. Not only is it inconvenient to wade in among your flowers to tend them, it's bad for the soil to be trampled on all the time and the flowers in the middle are too far away to be admired in close-up. These beds, which are about a metre and a half wide are about right: wide enough to give plenty of room for bulky growers such as these lavateras and watsonias, and narrow enough that they don't have to be walked on.

OPPOSITE: Here, a beautiful grass path curves between Japanese cherry trees underplanted with rich carpets of spring flowers. Grass is the ideal material for paths in a big garden; indeed, it is often the only choice, as paving on this scale is very expensive. It doesn't matter if it is less than perfect—do the few gaps, weeds and patches of moss spoil the beauty of the scene? In any case, few of us have the time or the paid help to do finicky grooming in such a large garden—there are too many other jobs such as watering, planting and keeping the grass from turning into an overgrown field.

INSTANT GARDENS

Gardeners tend to live in the future: trees take decades to grow to their full beauty, even a rose bush takes a couple of years to reach its peak, but what if you are renting or know that a career move will mean moving house in a year or three? You probably won't want to invest money in paving and structures, but you might be prepared to plant a few ultra-fast growing trees. There are surprisingly many: most acacias, some eucalypts and the very pretty (but frost-tender) *Virgilia capensis*. Bamboo can be planted full-size for instant screening, you can fill out the picture with shrub-sized annuals such as sunflowers, cleomes and cosmos—and vegetables come to harvest in a few weeks or months. If you are longing for some more permanent plants you may wish to try container gardening: that way you can take your plants with you when you move.

ABOVE: The pots themselves are an important element in the design of a potted garden. They need not all be as handsome as these, but they do need to be easy on the eye. Plastic rarely is, but timber, concrete and wood can be: and it is a good idea to stay with one or two materials. These ornate terracotta pots are a design traditionally used in Italy for lemon trees, one of the best fruit trees for container growing.

LEFT: A summer display of potted annuals, all in shades of blue, mauve and white—petunias, lobelias, a daisy or two, and some pansies left over from the spring contingent make a pretty display. When they fade, they will be replaced by others currently being grown out the back, and thus this important corner is kept in full bloom all year.

ABOVE: There is no soil available here: these gardens are actually on an inner-city footpath which cannot be dug up. So the entire show comes from potted plants, grown in containers sufficiently large to allow bamboo, bougainvilleas and an assortment of other shrubs to grow to something like their full size. Bigger pots dry out more slowly too, so they need less maintenance. Even so, you can't neglect a potted garden, especially in hot weather. The whole street shows what can happen when neighbours get together to beautify their environment.

LEFT: If you want to decorate the front of the house for a party or for Christmas, there is no easier or more effective way to do it than by arranging a few potted flowers. They can be taken elsewhere when the party is over, and if they are to be in their place for only a few days it doesn't matter if their temporary home would otherwise be too shady for them. Don't these pink and white petunias make a welcoming show on the front steps?

THE FUNCTIONAL GARDEN

There was a time when 'the garden' meant the ground in front of the house, embellished with trees and flowers for the delight of visitors. They didn't see the backyard—it was taken up with washing lines, outhouses, a vegetable patch and maybe a stable. The advent of plumbing, motor cars and dryers has freed the backyard to become the private outdoor 'living room' though we still need to find a place for the shed, the compost heap and maybe a place to grow vegetables and cut flowers. Each of these areas presents a different set of problems and opportunities and all should be considered when planning a garden.

The house is simple in style, and the front garden is too. On either side of the gravel path are groundcovers and simple perennial flowers. The basic symmetry is reinforced by the pot plants and the two standard azaleas. A splendid Japanese cherry canopies the garden with its autumn foliage. Notice how the blue-green of the window frames doesn't clash with the natural greens of the garden, leaving the front door to provide a focal point of bright colour.

FRONT GARDENS

The modern front garden serves as a kind of vestibule to the house itself. Its main duty is to provide a pleasing, safe passage from the street to the front door and to get the car from the street to the garage. Basically what is needed is a safe, well-lit path to the door. All else is ornament, but that ornament is important. A front garden should say 'welcome' to our visitors and, more importantly, to us when we come home at the end of the day. We might decide to set off the façade of the house with low plantings in the front and trees on either side, or we might decide to veil it lightly or heavily with planting.

These days we don't spend much time in our front garden as there is usually little space or privacy. Though we want it to look nice and enhance the neighbourhood, we don't want it to take up too much gardening time. Simple, easy-care plantings are the order of the day, and they can look as attractive as any.

LEFT: Where the front garden slopes, you cannot always make a direct approach to the house without your paths and drives being too steep for comfort. An oblique one, across the slope, is called for. This need not be a disadvantage: an off-centre first view can be flattering to the house (it usually makes it look larger), and it often allows you to arrange your plantings so that the full impact of the façade is only revealed at the last moment. A sloping path or drive needs a slight camber so that rainwater can run off to the side. This beautifully detailed gravel drive with its brick gutters is a fine example.

BEAUTIFYING THE STREET

The street itself is part of the approach to your house and there is often scope for beautifying it. If there are no street trees, lobby the council to have them planted; and if there is space between the fence and the footpath where some easy-care flowers could be grown without blocking public access, why not plant some? But don't choose something precious that you would grieve over if it were stolen or damaged.

LEFT: The need to provide access paths both to the front door for visitors and to the garage for the family car can complicate the design of the front garden. Which is to be given the emphasis? One way of solving the problem is to separate the drive from the rest of the garden with plantings so that it becomes a long 'hallway' in itself. A complete enclosure with head-high shrubs like this one is only possible where you have plenty of room, though even on an ordinary-sized lot you can achieve a similar effect with knee-high plants and maybe a strategically placed small tree or two.

ABOVE: Here a rather grand avenue of liquidambars leads up to an equally grand house. Avenue trees can be spaced rather closely as this encourages them to reach their branches out over the road.

PLANTS FOR
THE FRONT GARDEN

Old houses were often built with their floors high off the ground so the tradition developed of masking the bare wall below the ground floor windowsills with 'foundation planting'. If used wisely, this style of planting can still greatly enhance the appearance of a façade, even of a low-slung modern house: the simple band of green acts as a kind of dado. If the house is lumpish in proportion, extend the planting a little on either end to give the illusion of length; if it's tall and gaunt, a wide band of planting can bring it down to earth and link it with the garden as a whole.

As long as your chosen plants won't grow taller than the windowsills and block out the light and view, you can use any plants that please you and are suited to the aspect (shady or sunny). Shrubs such as kurume azaleas, lavender, rosemary, gardenias, diosmas, westringias; dramatic evergreen or semi-evergreen perennials such as acanthus, agapanthus, heliconias or *Euphorbia wulfenii*; ferns; or even bushy flowers such as busy lizzies, are all suitable.

ABOVE: Here the design of the front garden is determined by the formal architecture of the neo-Georgian house. Matched cypresses, matched urns with white flowers, matching plantings and shrubbery, all emphasise the symmetry of the rather grand entrance with its pilasters and Ionic entablature. It could all be a little overbearing, but the small brick-paved terrace is a friendly touch as it allows space for a small group of people to gather as they arrive and when they are saying their good-byes. This is important for any house; nothing is more uncomfortable than a crowded front step.

OPPOSITE TOP: Where local ordinances preclude a front fence, creating an effective entrance from the street can be a problem. Here it has been solved by the simplest means: a narrow bed planted with agapanthus divides the property from the street, and a stone letter box crowned with a ball suggests a gateway. It also provides a place to display the house number where visitors can easily find it. (Driving around an unfamiliar street at night looking for half-hidden numbers is a frustrating but common experience.)

OPPOSITE BOTTOM: The old-fashioned circular driveway had a practical purpose—it allowed carriages to drop their passengers at the front door and go out again without the horses having to walk backwards. These days it can still make an impressive approach to a house, but as it needs to have an outside diameter of at least 14 m—more if you plan to allow people to park on it—it is really only feasible on the largest suburban estates or, as here, in the country.

LIVING AREAS

The outdoor 'living room', like the one indoors, should be spacious and comfortable. It needs to be private, which means that it will almost certainly be in the back garden, away from the street. You need shade in summer, sun in winter; and you need a comfortable 'floor' for all seasons. This means paving, at least next to the house—and if that can lead onto a lawn for the children to play on, so much the better. Consider whether you want your furniture to be permanent or would you rather bring it out from the garage as needed? The same is true of the barbecue; a permanent, built-in one or a portable? Do you want swings and slides for the children? And of course, lighting; without it you can't use the garden in the evening and there is certainly nothing more pleasant than spending an evening outdoors with friends.

ABOVE: This delightfully rustic fireplace for cool spring and autumn evenings certainly fits in beautifully with the highly informal style of the garden and suggests the usual stove-like designs for barbecues are not the only possibilities for cooking outside. LEFT: This brick paved patio substantially extends the living space of the house. The planting is entirely of Australian native plants, whose soft olives and greys are in perfect harmony with the earth tones of the bricks. Built in the same brick as the steps, the barbecue extends their line: indeed its back wall serves as part of the retaining wall for the upper level.

ABOVE: With its emphasis on rectangular lines and structures, this garden is perhaps more a piece of outdoor architecture than gardening: flowers play a distinctly secondary role to the formal pools and columns. But imagine how dull the garden would be without them! The whole effect is of elegant formality, a setting for sipping champagne to the sound of a string quartet, perhaps, rather than an informal Sunday barbecue. Yet it is not the whole garden, and it derives much of its impact from the way it links the house to the wider setting of informal plantings and glimpses of the countryside beyond.

LIGHTING THE GARDEN

Lighting the garden can be a difficult task. A moonlit garden has its own special beauty and you don't want to spoil it by flooding the garden with bright light; on the other hand, you don't want to be stumbling around in the dark. Paths leading to the front door, steps and places where you sit out after dark need to be lit up sufficiently for safety. As a general rule, the more discreet your light fittings, the better; you don't want them calling attention to themselves during the day, though there are more ornate styles available that can look as attractive as a piece of sculpture, displayed against a green backdrop. Happily, most gardens lend themselves to traditional styles like this lantern, half-hidden by day among the foliage. Make sure that all your electrical connections are perfectly waterproof—rain and electricity are a potentially lethal combination!

ABOVE: Playground equipment is an investment with a limited life, as children grow out of it surprisingly fast, but if you decide to have it, there are a few points to consider. Almost everything here—the cubby house, the steps, the swing frames—is made of preservative-treated pine logs, and building it would certainly not be beyond the skill of most home carpenters. All is neatly and compactly arranged and set on a generous area of deep sand (many experts would prefer a 15 cm layer of tanbark) to cushion the inevitable falls and spills. Shade is essential too, to avoid problems with skin cancer later on. Here it is provided simply by climbing roses growing on the swing structure—but might something without thorns have been preferable?

LEFT: While a spa can be placed in a secluded spot in the garden almost like an ornamental pond, a sauna really needs to be enclosed in a small building, traditionally of timber. It needs to be placed so that it is handy to a swimming pool for the obligatory cold plunge when you have had enough steam. This sauna is in a country garden and has the luxury of a small lake nearby—you can glimpse it beautifully framed by the gate posts and the tree. The awkward slope down to the entrance to the sauna house has been elegantly handled by creating a semi-circular terrace on which tables and chairs can be placed for outdoor living.

The summer house or gazebo is a Victorian idea which is enjoying new popularity. It need not be as elaborately styled as this one, which was designed to complement a rather grand Victorian house—all that is needed is a roof to keep the sun and rain off, posts to support it, and a seat or two to sit on. How you assemble them, and whether you adorn the structure with climbing roses or other creepers, is entirely up to you. (If you don't feel up to the task of design, several companies make prefabricated gazebo kits.) But do place it where it will command a pleasant view, either over surrounding country or of the garden itself.

WORK AREAS

A well-planned gardening shed can really add to the pleasure of gardening. It is amazing how delightful it is not to have to rummage in a pile of junk to find the spade or to have to untangle the rake from a stack of dahlia stakes.

Just how big the shed should be depends on how much equipment you have: you need room for the lawn-mower, for large tools, for bags of fertiliser and potting mix plus a spacious work bench. You might like a medicine cupboard to store chemicals out of harm's way—and you'll almost certainly find homeless junk from the house drifting into the shed too. If you give the shed a small yard of its own, you can put the compost heap there and store firewood too. Supply it with electricity, add a secure lock on the door and you'll have created a 'garden work centre', not just a 'shed'.

ABOVE: You still occasionally find the old outhouse, now superseded by indoor plumbing, standing at the bottom of old gardens. This one has been doubled in size to serve as the garden shed, its nondescript architecture and cheap materials entirely obliterated by smothering it in ivy and creeping fig. Some may object that the creepers will attract spiders and other creepy-crawlies, but so long as the little building is given an adequate window and cleaned out occasionally they should give no trouble. LEFT: Nowadays most of us keep our gardening equipment in the garage and a special shed is a luxury, but a pleasantly designed shed can do double duty as a pleasing focal point in the garden. This is an old one on a country property and is pleasing in its rough-hewn antiquity. The Virginia creeper looks romantic and won't do any harm to the walls so long as they are sound. Indeed it (and ivy) can help to preserve old walls by keeping them dry.

LEFT: A walled garden for cut flowers, vegetables and fruit was the pride of many a great establishment in days gone by. This is a rustic version, scaled to the modern pocket with its high grey timber fences instead of masonry walls. Here between the paths of recycled bluestone, are beds generous enough to supply all the cut flowers you could desire, and all the vegetables and herbs too. And this is no mere shed but a garden work centre, with ample space for all the stakes, bags of fertiliser, pots and tools the gardener needs. You could re-create this scene in an average-sized backyard, especially if you could 'borrow' the trees next door as a backdrop.

BELOW: This potting shed, with its latticed walls is a grand example of what our grandparents called a 'bush house', in which they used to grow the exotic plants we now use as house plants, all of which need shade and shelter from drying winds. If you replaced the roof with a closely spaced lattice or with semi-transparent fibreglass to let in more light it would be a perfect home for a collection of orchids or bonsai trees.

You can't garden without tools, but you don't need gadgets. The wheelbarrow and garden fork have not changed in their basic design for centuries, despite the advent of modern materials like steel and plastic. (The Romans made their fork tines and spade blades of bronze.) Notice the strong canvas bag with its pockets for secateurs, string and odds and ends. It is almost a portable shed in itself, and would make an ideal Christmas present for the gardener who has everything.

MAKING A COMPOST BIN

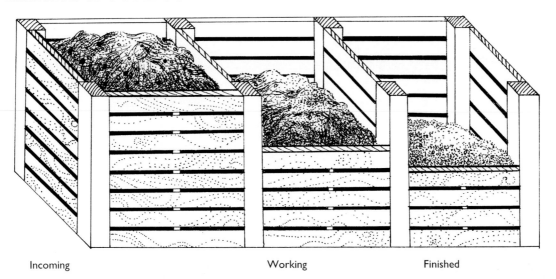

Incoming   Working   Finished

This is the compost maker's dream—a triple bin, in timber, with removable fronts. If each is 1 m square and high, the outfit will be adequate for all but the very largest gardens. The point of having three is that while one is being filled, one is maturing, and the third is ready for use. When that is emptied, you can pitchfork the half-ripe compost from the second into it, thus 'turning' it and ensuring even rotting.

ABOVE: Every garden should have its compost heap where all the organic rubbish is recycled into the best fertiliser and soil improver there is. Some keen gardeners discuss recipes for compost over the dinner table, but you don't want to see the heap every time you go out into the garden, any more than you want to see the washing machine, no matter how fashion-conscious you might be. This is the basic model—a pile under an out-of-the-way tree which shelters it from getting too wet when it rains—but you can create elaborate arrangements of open bins in timber or brick, or closed ones of plastic.

PRODUCTIVE GARDENS

Growing vegetables is as much fun as growing shrubs and flowers. More so, some gardeners say—you have the added pleasure of eating them. So why are they usually shunted off to a corner where they won't be seen? Surely we still don't hold to the Victorian idea that only the poor grew their own? If planned properly, a neat, well-maintained vegetable patch offers some beautiful harmonies of form and colour. The problem is that just as everything is looking great you have to spoil it by harvesting. (It's the same with cut flowers.) The solution to this is simple: by adding paving or neatly maintained grass areas between the beds or edging them with something low and more permanent such as parsley, rosemary or lavender, your vegetable garden will remain pleasing to the eye, even after harvesting.

LEFT: Though it rarely shows much in the way of flowers—few vegetables except the scarlet runner bean offer much in this department—a beautifully maintained vegetable garden can be very satisfying to the eye. And if you want to study the possibilities of green, this is the place to do it—just about every vegetable offers a different shade. True, there are some (like tomatoes) that look a little scruffy but these beets, cabbages and lettuces, set against a backdrop of climbing peas, are as handsome as many an exotic but inedible foliage plant.

WHAT TO GROW?

It seems obvious enough, but you'd be surprised how often people forget: only grow the vegetables that your family enjoys eating. If they loathe, say, spinach, the sight of you proudly bringing in an armload won't make them change their minds. Nor should you grow too much, even of the family favourites, or you'll soon be hearing: 'Oh no, not that again!'

ABOVE: One half of this backyard is given over to lawn, surrounded by shrubs, the other half to a vegetable garden. The arrangement of the vegetable patch is simplicity itself: straight brick paths surround and give access to a series of rectangular beds in which vegetables are casually mixed with flowers for cutting—Russell lupins and a rose bush or three. Fruit trees, mainly apples, stand to one side, and a grape vine (not yet in leaf when this picture was taken in early spring) shelters the back door.

ABOVE: The Victorians were very fond of arranging fancy-shaped beds on the lawn and filling them with low-growing flowers or coloured-leaved plants, in a style called 'carpet bedding'. In this modern example, vegetables take the place of flowers; the many shades and textures of green, grey and bronze create quite a splendid effect. On a practical note, the vegetables are getting all the sun they need, and the grass paths make it easy to gain access for tending and harvesting them.

ABOVE: The beauty of any garden resides as much in its details as in the big picture. Here we see the purple-leaved sage, just as good for stuffing the roast duck as the ordinary grey-leaved one, in charming contrast with the flower buds of the green-leaved lavender cotton, *Santolina virens* (the usual one, *S. chamaecyparissus*, has grey leaves) and a fancy-leaved lettuce. Some gardeners shun the ordinary forms of plants, preferring unusual ones like these.

TOP LEFT: Herbs are fascinating as much for their historical associations as for their fragrance and flavour, but though an assortment can look charming when seen in close-up like this, they are often rather shapeless growers (some would be rude enough to say 'weedy'), and the traditional formal herb garden, centred on a sundial or statue, was invented partly to overcome this. The pattern of the paths dividing the beds imposes a degree of order, similar to the way a heavy gilt frame can keep an abstract painting from looking a mess.

BOTTOM LEFT: Roses and cabbages! What would milady say? Yet this vignette is just what the old-fashioned cottage garden was about—every inch of ground was made to produce something of use, either herbs, vegetables or flowers to adorn the house. Looked at without snobbery, don't the broad grey leaves of the cabbages set off the cream and pink flowers of the 'Peace' rose beautifully? Half the art of gardening is learning to see the beauty in unexpected combinations of plants such as these.

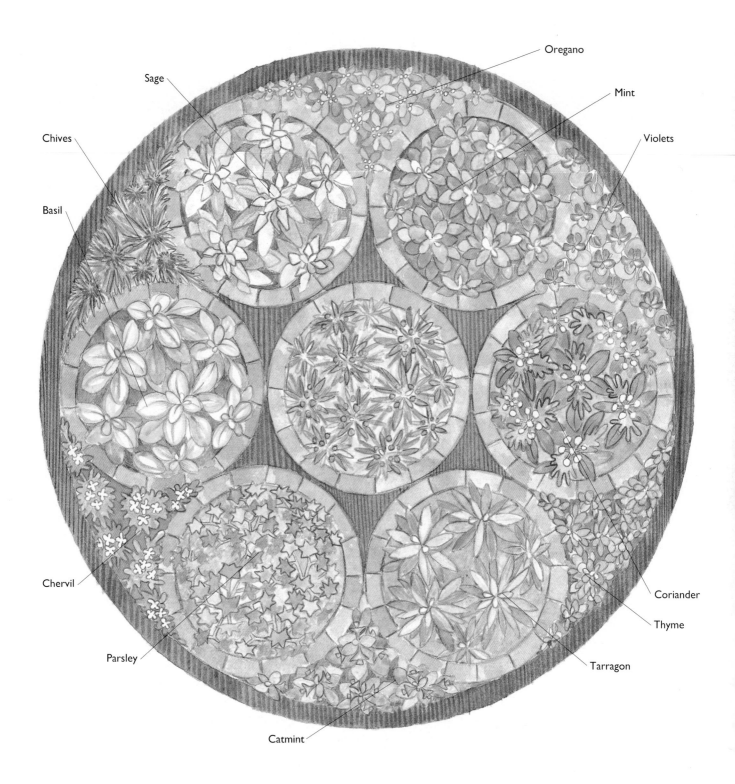

Oregano

Sage

Mint

Chives

Violets

Basil

Chervil

Coriander

Thyme

Parsley

Tarragon

Catmint

PLANNING A HERB GARDEN

Here is a pretty adaptation of a Tudor 'knot', as the patterned beds of herbs fashionable in those days were called. In a modern garden it would make a pretty focal point for a lawn or patio. Each circle is outlined in bricks (as is the whole thing) and you can raise them a little above the general level of the bed for a three-dimensional effect if you want to. Adjust the sizes to suit the space available but don't make it all too big or the centre will be out of comfortable reach. Anything from 60 to 90 cm is about right for each circle. Choose any herbs you fancy, putting the tallest in the centre and using the lowest to fill in at the edges.

INDEX

Published by Murdoch Books®, a division of Murdoch Magazines Pty Ltd,
213 Miller Street, North Sydney NSW 2060

Managing Editor, Craft & Gardening: Christine Eslick
Editor: Kim Rowney
Designer: Michèle Lichtenberger
Photographs: Lorna Rose (all unless specified otherwise); Murdoch Books® Picture Library (50 L, 75, 100 R);
C. Betteridge (62 T); Keith Manns (68 R); Reg Morrison (53 bottom); Ray Joyce (88 top, 89 top)
Illustrator: Mia Fawcett
CEO & Publisher: Anne Wilson
International Sales Director: Mark Newman

National Library of Australia Cataloguing-in-Publication Data
Mann, Roger. Making beautiful gardens
Includes index. ISBN 0 86411 596 2. 1. Gardens—Design. 2. Gardening. I. Title. 635
Printed by Prestige Litho, Queensland
© Text, design, commissioned photography and illustrations Murdoch Books® 1997

Acknowledgements
The publisher thanks the following for allowing photography in their gardens: Mr & Mrs Anderson, Wahroonga NSW (27 R, 39); Ashcombe
Maze, Shoreham Vic. (35 bottom L); Helmut Bakaitus, Leura NSW (105 top); V. Berger, Canberra ACT (11 top L); Bringalbit, Sidonia Vic. (59
top, 84, 87 bottom); Burnbank, Wagga Wagga NSW (87 top, 95 bottom); Buskers End, Bowral NSW (4, 15 top, 46 top R, 52 R); Mr & Mrs
Andrew Cannon, Manildra NSW (102); Cheplakwet, Moss Vale NSW (53 top); Cherry Cottage, Mt Wilson NSW (11 top R, 32 top L, 41
bottom, 85); Dr & Mrs Chi, Glenorie NSW (37 top, 78 top); Convent Gallery, Daylesford Vic. (inside front cover, 35 bottom R, 59 bottom
L); Country Farm Perennials Nursery, Nayook Vic. (55 bottom R); Craigie Lea, Leura NSW (16 L, 24 R, 83 bottom, 90, 96 top); Crosshills,
Otorohanga NZ (15 bottom, 37 bottom, 46 top L); Mr & Mrs Davey, Castlemaine Vic. (64, 73 bottom); Dunedin, St Leonards Tas. (8 L, 9, 61
top, 92); Eryldene, Gordon NSW (20 L, 21 bottom, 28 L, 38 R, 74 L); Everglades, Leura NSW (27 L); Fairyburn, Orange NSW (29, 41 top);
Mr & Mrs Fitzpatrick, Lane Cove NSW (74 R); Foxglove Spires, Tilba Tilba NSW (5, 55 top, 81, 97 top, back cover); Gladstone House,
Beechworth Vic. (54); Mary Glasson, Molong NSW (cover, 21 top, 36 L, 59 bottom R, 99); Mr & Mrs Gray, Wahroonga NSW (26, 97
bottom); Heronswood, Dromana Vic. (11 bottom, 14 R, 45, 46 bottom, 58, 105 bottom); Hillview, Exeter NSW (31 centre, 36 R, 93 top);
Mrs Hilyard, Canberra ACT (38 L, 55 bottom L); Tina & John Howie, Orange NSW (50 R, 101 bottom); John Hunt, Kenthurst NSW (96
bottom); Jaara Farm, Barkers Creek Vic. (100 L); Mrs B. Jenkins, Ryde NSW (101 top); Val & Doug Jones, Neerim Vic. (98 top); Kennerton
Green, Mittagong NSW (22 top, 52 L, 86, 106 R); Kewarra Beach Resort, Cairns Qld (83 top); Paul Koller, Leura NSW (8 R); Lambruk,
Fryerstown Vic. (20 R, 31 top); Pat & Selwyn Lawrence, Hunterville NZ (88 bottom); Lindfield Park, Mt Irvine NSW (17); Margaret Martin,
Wahroonga NSW (18 bottom); Mayday Hills Hospital, Beechworth, Vic. (66 top); Merry Garth, Mt Wilson NSW (76 R); Kathie & Arthur
Mills, Orange NSW (70); Raylee & Gavin Muir, Te Awamutu NZ (106 bottom L); Mr & Mrs Mullen, Pymble NSW (94); Mt Tomah, NSW
Botanic Gardens (35 top); Debbie Nock, Crows Nest NSW (89 bottom); Ruth Osborne, Beecroft NSW (78 bottom); Polly & Peter Park,
Canberra ACT (44, 68 L, 69 top); Pinehill, Castlemaine Vic. (103); Plassy, Pipers Creek Vic. (31 bottom); Jenny & Shane Porteus, Medlow Bath
NSW (34); Quincey Cottage, Medlow Bath NSW (106 top L, 49 bottom); Rathmoy, Hunterville NZ (32 bottom L, 98 bottom); D. & F. Rex,
Mossman Qld (76 L, 79 bottom); Janet & Lee Rowan, Newcastle NSW (69 bottom); Royal Botanic Gardens, Sydney NSW (62 bottom); Mary
Rutledge, Longford Tas. (10); Felicity Say, Castlemaine Vic. (57 top); Maggie Shepherd, Canberra ACT (18 top, 22 bottom, 23, 40, 47, 65 top,
65 bottom); Swane's Nursery, Dural NSW (71 top L, 71 top R, 71 centre L, 71 centre R, 79 centre); Talwood, Frenchs Forest NSW (28 R);
The Folly, Chewton Vic. (16 R, 24 L, 61 bottom, 73 top); The Rose Cottage, Beechworth Vic. (66 bottom); Ann Thomson Garden Advisory
Service, St Ives NSW (63); Joan Thompson, Orange NSW (30); Titoki Point, Taihape NZ (48, 67, 80); A. & R. Tonkin, Orange NSW (60, 71
bottom); Tour de Malakoff Rose Nursery, Beechworth Vic. (19 R); Tregamere, Te Awamutu NZ (104); Welby Garden Centre, Southern
Highlands Challenge Foundation, Welby NSW (19 L); Deirdre Williamson, Church Point NSW (49 top, 77); Woodleigh Farm Garden, Marton
NZ (12); Woodlyn Nurseries, Five Ways Vic. (57 centre L, 57 centre R); Yengo, Mt Wilson NSW (14 L, 42).
A number of the gardens photographed in this book are open under Australia's Open Garden Scheme.

Front cover: The 'Orange Triumph' rose plus an assortment of climbing roses line the path
Back cover: Flowering plum, narcissus and geums
Inside front cover: *Campanula persicifolia*, delphiniums, Mexican daisies, lavender, buddleias and *Lychnis coronaria*
Title page: Old-fashioned or heritage rose